ISBN 978-1-334-27501-2
PIBN 10761045

A PEEP
INSIDE

P U B L I S H E D   B Y
MONTGOMERY WARD & CO.
C H I C A G O ,   U .   S .   A .

THE World's Oldest and Largest Catalogue House.....
The House That Tells the Truth......The House
That Guarantees Satisfaction on Everything and Keeps
Every Promise.....The House Whose Name Stands for
Quality.....The House Whose Prices Are the Lowest.....

JUST A PEEP

In this little book we have done the best we could to give you a peep—a glance—just an inkling of the thousands of good things to be found within the covers of our new catalogue No. 73.

We have gone through the big book and picked out the goods we are selling by the carloads; the goods your friends are buying, your neighbors are buying, everybody is buying. We are filling their orders by the thousands. These popular goods are reproduced in this book for your benefit.

If for some reason or other you have neglected sending for our Catalogue 73, we now offer you in these pages one more opportunity to get it, packed free of charge with your shipment ordered from this book.

OUR CATALOGUE 73, EDITION DE LUXE

is without doubt or argument THE LARGEST, HEAVIEST, HANDSOMEST, GREATEST MONEY SAVING CATALOGUE EVER PRINTED. **IT WEIGHS ALMOST 6 POUNDS.**

It is about twice as heavy as any catalogue ever before published by Montgomery Ward & Co., or any other firm.

It is the only 1904-5 Catalogue quoting practically EVERYTHING you or any member of your family will need during the next year. No more sending for special catalogues (clothing samples excepted)— the big book contains quotations on our entire stock.

It is printed on fine, heavy paper, which makes the illustrations print clearly — a delight to the most critical eye.

It quotes a larger stock than ever before.

AND THE PRICES ARE THE LOWEST, as usual, quality considered.

This handsome, heavy edition of our Catalogue (our Edition de Luxe) is too heavy to be sent profitably by mail or express, so we are going to make it possible for you to get one by freight, free of charge.

On the following pages we print an assortment of Groceries used by every American family. You MUST buy them sometime, somewhere. If you will send us your order for this Grocery lot now, we will not only save you 15 to 20 per cent

on the cost, but will include three presents (one of them our Edition de Luxe Catalogue), which will be worth more to you than the amount you send us for the groceries.

If you don't want the groceries, order something else from this book — the Edition de Luxe will be packed free with your shipment.

This is undoubtedly the greatest opportunity we have ever offered you.

Will you take it?

Of course, if you don't want this fine large Catalogue, you may send us 15 cents, same as you've always done, and we will send you our 3-lb. (mailing size) STANDARD or regular Edition of Catalogue 73. This Edition is not so handsome as the Edition de Luxe, but contains the same number of pages (almost 1200) printed on thinner paper, same as our previous catalogues have been printed on. Our Standard Edition is far ahead of any catalogue ever printed by any other firm.

If you want the Standard Edition by return mail, send us 15 cents with the coupon herewith:

-------------------------------- CUT OFF HERE --------------------------------

CUT OFF HERE

FOLD HERE

FOLD HERE

FOLD HERE

FOLD HERE

Fold on the dotted lines and drop a nickel and a dime or fifteen cents in stamps in pocket

Standard Edition

Standard size, standard weight, standard paper. Send 15 cents in stamps or coin to partially pay the postage and we will send a copy free, postpaid. The actual postage is over 30 cents, and the cost of the catalogue is almost a dollar; but if you will send 15 cents, to show that you are acting in good faith, we will gladly meet you more than half way and forward a catalogue, all charges paid — 15 cents in stamps or coin is all we ask from you. We will supply the difference.

MONTGOMERY WARD & CO.:

Enclosed find 15c. for partial postage or expressage on Catalogue No. 73. Please send to

Name----

P. O..

R. F. D. Route----

State----

Be sure to enclose this Coupon in envelope.

Our Liberal Grocery Offer

We offer here an assortment of Groceries, practically **every** item of which is used by every family. (See list and prices on second page following.) At these prices, and with the presents which go with each assortment, the entire lot is yours at less than your dealer could buy it for at wholesale.

Why we Make this Liberal Offer:

There are three reasons for it: The first is, that we wish to acquaint you with our low prices on good Groceries. To this end, we are offering these valuable presents as a means of introduction—to make you acquainted with our splendid Grocery values.

Secondly, there are many little items elsewhere in this booklet which you no doubt will want to buy, but which would cost you more by mail or express than by freight. By ordering this Grocery lot, these other articles can be added, the entire shipment going by freight, at a cost of almost nothing per item for transportation.

The third reason: we want you to send us an order heavy enough to be shipped profitably by freight, so we can include a free copy of the largest and best catalogue ever published.

The Important Point to Remember

Our customers are fast learning to have their orders shipped by freight. This means cheapest transportation, and therefore lowest cost for the entire order delivered at your station.

Of course, there are very few things you will want that cannot be shipped alone by mail or express and still save you money. But why not ship by freight and save more?

This is very easy when you remember that we sell EVERYTHING you use or need. A freight shipment should weigh at least 100 lbs. When you see anything advertised that you would like to order, turn to our catalogue and buy it at the lowest price. Then, instead of ordering the single item by mail or express, order something else which will soon be needed by some member of your family, and the entire order can come by freight for what the single item would cost by express.

See the Point?

The great secret of our low prices and success lies in the fact that our customers can supply ALL their wants from our Catalogue at Wholesale Prices, and thus ship by freight with lowest transportation charges.

And even these low freight charges can be still further reduced by asking a neighbor to join you in ordering in the same shipment and divide the freight with you, making it practically nothing for each.

See List of
Items on next
page—

How we can Make this Offer:

We want you to have our new Catalogue No. 73, Edition de Luxe — the largest, handsomest, and best Catalogue ever published.

We believe you know a bargain when you see one, and will therefore take advantage of this Grocery offer. If you are far-seeing enough to order this Bargain Grocery Lot, we are willing to forego our usual profit for this one time in order that you shall receive one of these catalogues, absolutely free of charge.

If you had a bushel of peaches for sale you could afford to give one away in order to sell the bushel, couldn't you?

Where we Get Even

is in the circulation of our Catalogues. We want to send out as many as we can, for every catalogue brings us an order, and every order makes a permanent customer for us.

[See next page for description of Grocery Offer.]

$4.78

COMPLETE

Our Great Bargain Grocery Lot No. 100

See Illustration on preceding page

This is in many respects one of the greatest offers we ever made. Never before have we offered presents the value of which is positively as much as the price of the entire order, thus virtually giving you 2 for 1. We have made immense preparations for the landslide of orders which we know will come. Goods have been ordered in car-load lots, for we believe the people know a good thing when they see it and we expect an order from every person who gets one of these books.

The groceries which bear our own name and brands are first-class in every respect. We want you to try them. Every item in this lot is subject to our liberal guarantee and can be returned at our expense if not satisfactory and money refunded. Order the Complete Assortment, we will not fill orders for separate items. Order Lot No. 100. Write today and secure prompt shipment.

This offer good only until Nov. 30, 1904.

10 lbs. Snap (Roasted) Coffee—a real snap.............$1.70
> Snap Coffee consists of the small beans sifted from high grade coffees that sell at wholesale for 25 and 30 cents per pound. You will be pleased with the quality. The only reason we can sell Snap Coffee so cheaply is because the size of the berries is too small to meet the requirements of the expensive grades.

10 lbs. Michigan Hand Picked Navy Beans. .... .33
> Excellent goods at a very moderate price. Nutritive value considered, beans make one of the very cheapest articles of diet.

9-lb. Sack Rolled Oats (1904 crop)..... .... .30
> Fresh Milled from 1904 Crop Oats. No old and stale packages. We have no "left overs." The oatmeal breakfast is the muscle builder and strength sustainer.

5-lbs. Fancy Japan Rice (Whole Berry)............. .25
> XXX Grade. One of the most nutritious foods you can buy. Our price saves you 50 per cent on equal quality.

1-lb. Can M. W. & Co.'s Pure Cream of Tarter Baking Powder.. .33
> Our Baking Powder is equal to any high priced Baking Powder sold and our price is 25 per cent cheaper than advertised brands. We are giving you an excellent opportunity to learn how much you've been paying for an advertised name.

½-lb. Cake M. W. & Co.'s Premium Chocolate.......... .14
> This is the season when you want Chocolate for Iceing purposes. Don't give the children too much coffee; Chocolate is much more nutritious and better for them.

10-Bars Hannah Cobb's Pure Laundry Soap.... .... .40
> This fine Home Made Family Soap has been a great favorite with our customers for years. It is equal to all and superior to many 5 cent soaps on the market.

3 6-oz. Cakes M. W. & Co.'s White Floating Soap.... .15
> For toilet and bath. Strictly high grade in every way. You will find our White Floating Soap to be very superior, the maximum in size and quality at the minimum price.

2½-pt. Bottles Hannah Cobb's Home Made Catsup........ .24
> Something every family uses. The most nutritious condiment and aid to digestion you can put on your table. New 1904 Catsup, made from red ripe tomatoes, nicely spiced, the finest catsup on the market.

3 1-lb. Packages Fancy Seeded Raisins................ .24
> Raisins as an article of diet are worth double their price. They are system regulators and should be eaten with much greater frequency than they are. A rice pudding mixed plentifully with raisins makes a most excellent and healthful dish. These are the best quality Muscatel Raisins, freshly seeded and every package is full weight. This is a good opportunity to try them.

2 1-lb. Packages M. W. & Co.'s Corn Starch. $0.10
> You will be delighted with our Corn Starch. Selected quality, absolutely pure and wholesome.

2 No. 2 Size Cans Fancy 1904 Corn..................... .20
2 No. 2 " " " 1904 Early June Peas.......... .20
2 No. 3 " " " 1904 Whole Tomatoes .... .20
> The Corn, Peas and Tomatoes that we furnish in this lot are the better grades, in regular size cans. They are quickly prepared and handy when unexpected company arrives. We could sell you cheaper grades but are listing here the quality preferred by the vast majority of our customers.

Total for this Excellent Assortment............$4.78

The same quality of goods would cost you at retail about $6.00.

PRESENT No. 1—Handsome Sanitary Bread and Cake Box (See illustration on preceding page) value, $3.50. FREE
> Manufacturers retail price, $3.50 each. A very necessary and convenient pantry accessory. It is 20 inches high, 19 inches wide, and 14 inches deep, made of heavy plate tin, beautifully japanned and decorated. The two shelves can be removed, and the front opens down, which makes the cleaning of the inside a very simple matter.

PRESENT No. 2—1 Book of 200 Recipes for preparing Rice, one of our most nutritious, easily digested and cheapest articles of diet. A very useful book.......FREE

PRESENT No. 3—Catalogue 73, Edition De Luxe..:.:..FREE
> Not counting the large Catalogue which costs us almost a Dollar each, the retail value of this entire lot, including the Presents, would be just about $10.00 in round figures. But to introduce our excellent Grocery Values more thoroughly and give you an opportunity to get our fine Edition De Luxe Catalogue absolutely FREE, we make this entire lot at a price which we cannot see how you can afford to overlook, inasmuch as you will no doubt soon buy these items at higher prices from your local dealer if you don't send us your order now.

Order Lot No. 100, $10.00 retail value for only.............

$4.78

Weight of entire lot, 100 lbs.

CIGARS AND TOBACCOS

POPULAR FAVORITES AT POPULAR PRICES.
We do not sample cigars, nor do we sell less than a box.

☞ Keep cigars in a moist place, and they will give much better satisfaction.

Cheroots and Stogies.

AE904—Genuine Wheeling Stogies, pk'd 100 in round b'x.
Per box........ $1.16
Per 1,000....... 10.60

AE906—Old Virginia Cheroots, packed 250 in box.
Per box......... $3.25
Per 1,000........ 12.50

AE908—Havana Stogies, 100 in box. The best thing made.
Per box........ $1.60
Per 1,000........ 14.50

AB910—General Arthur Operas, a small, fine flavored cigar. Come packed 10 cigars in a neat case; 10 cases in a box.
Price per box of 100 cigars....$1.25
Per 1,000.......... $11.80

AE912—Royal Bengal, little cigars, 10 in package, packed 100 in box. Price per box...............$1.25
Per 1,000........... 12.00

Smoking Tobacco

AE982—M.W. & Co.'s Sure Thing Smoking, the best cheap smoking tobacco on the market, 3½-oz. and ½-lb. packages, 30-lb. cases, per lb....18 Single lb....19

Holiday Candies

One-fourth Saving.

We offer you the following variety of candies at a saving to you of 25 per cent. Look over the list. You can buy lots of candy with very little money.

AE79—Sunshine Kisses, assorted flavors and very best quality. Put up in fancy decorated 3-lb. cans. Per can................................$0.68

AE80—Trowbridge's Twentieth Century Chocolate Chips—finest made—about 200 chips in a 5-lb. box. Per box................................ 1.25

AE81—Perfection Caramels, new style, unwrapped and packed in layers on tin partitions—assortment consists of Maple, Chocolate Almonds, Strawberry and Vanilla Walnut in each box.
1-lb. box for.................... .19
5-lb. box for.................... .86

AE82—Tower Top Holiday Mixture, clean, hard goods—suitable for Xmas entertainments and refilling of small boxes. 30-lb. pails for............ 2.50
50-lb. pails for................. 3.80
100-lb. boxes for............... 7.50

AE83—Tower Brand Sunset Mixture, contains Chocolate, Fine Dips, Creams, Jellies with slice of Pineapple on top. 10-lb. box for........... 1.50

AE84—Parisian Assorted Ices and Creams, large pieces. 10-lb. box for................. 1.10

AE85—Peerless Mixture, suitable for filling Xmas stockings—consists of Jelly Beans, Imperials, Baked Beans, Lady Kisses, etc. 5-lb. box for.... .50
30-lb. pail for............... 2.40

AE 1504—Mixed Nuts.

All 1904 crop, our own mixture and the best quality of each variety of nuts.
5½-lb. boxes, per lb.,...................$0.13
25-lb. boxes, per lb...................... .13½
5-lb. bag for............................ .72

Stock and Poultry Food

AE836—M.W. & Co.'s Horse and Cattle Powders,
6-lb. packages....................................$0.46
Per dozen packages............................. 5.00
AE838—Cracked Bone for Poultry, 25-lb. sacks.... .50
50-lb. sacks.................................... 1.00
100-lb. sacks.................................. 1.90
AE840—Raw Bone Meal, for cattle and poultry,
25-lb. sacks................................... .50
50-lb. sacks................................... 1.00
100-lb. sacks.................................. 1.90
AE842—Ground Oyster Shells, for poultry. 100-lb. sacks... .46
AE844—Mica Crystal Grits, for poultry. 100-lb. sacks... .52
AE847—Blatchford's Calf Meal, 20-lb. sacks...... .95
50-lb. sacks................................... 1.95
100-lb. sacks.................................. 3.90

Pure Ground Beef Scraps, for Poultry

FOR FATTENING.
AE850—25-lb. sacks..............................$0.65
50-lb. sacks................................... 1.20
100-lb. sacks.................................. 2.25

EGG PRODUCER.
AE851—Beef Meal, for poultry, the great egg producer, composed of beef, Bone and Blood.
25-lb. sacks...................................$0.52
50-lb. sacks................................... .98
100-lb. sacks.................................. 1.90
200-lb. sacks.................................. 3.75

Poultry Food

AE858—A mixture of selected stock. Corn, oats, Kaffir corn, millet, wheat, etc.
100-lb. sacks. Per sack....................... $1.75

5⁷⁵ A Clothing Harvest

We have been successful in securing a lot of men's suits from eastern manufacturers, at prices which, with a small margin added to cover cost of handling and filling of orders, will allow you to own them at one-third off our regular prices. We thus keep factories going during dull season, the manufacturer being willing to sell us a certain number of garments at cost, and oftentimes less, to keep his organization together. This also applies to our own force of employes, as sales of this kind, though not directly profitable in dollars and cents, enable us to keep valuable and experienced clerks in place of laying them off during this, the usual dull season. Order now to secure the pick of the season and just the size you desire. Sizes of the three following lots:

Men's Round Cut Sack Suits for $5⁷⁵

Same style as illustration. 35 to 44 chest. 30 to 42 waist. 30 to 36 inseam. No larger or smaller, longer or shorter.

Men's Sack Suits, an assorted lot, consisting of our celebrated plain Black Tubbers, easily worth $8.00 per suit. All wool Pebble Cheviots, plain black but rather rough surface or pebble effect, retail price, $10.00. Medium light gray small check, all wool Cassimeres, regular retail price, $8.00. These suits are all nicely and well made, with good quality of either serge or Italian body lining and good grade of trimmings throughout. Most of them have haircloth shape-retaining fronts. All are guaranteed satisfactory and extraordinary value or money refunded with transportation charges. They are medium in weight. Mention first and second choice.

WE 38 This suit.. $5.75

Men's Fine Dress Gloves for $1⁴⁰

WE 8907 Men's extra fine quality, unlined kid gloves, prix seams, quirk fingers, raised corded fancy silk stitched backs, snap fasteners. The stock is medium weight, made especially for us to meet a very large demand we have had for an English walking glove, in an assortment of the newest shades of tan. Pair $1.40

Round Cut
Sack Style

Suits made of tailoring fabrics at half price 7⁵⁰ Per Suit

These fabrics are all cassimere and cheviote, full heavy weights for Winter wear, and the patterns consist of dark and medium gray, dark and medium brown, and a few dark blue mixed effects. They are all of splendid quality, none sold for less than $10.50, and from that up to $12.50. All are well made with heavy double warp Italian body lining and fine sateen sleeve lining and genuine haircloth shape-retaining fronts and stylishly cut and well made by our own cutters and tailors during the dull season. We have a big lot of them, but when these are gone there will be no more. When ordering, mention which you prefer, medium or dark gray mixed, medium or dark brown mixed, or dark blue mixed, and we will send you nearest possible to your description. Send today and obtain best value ever sold for this price. Cut in round sack style.

WE 40. Weight, about 6 lbs................................. $7.50

$12 Fancy W'rst'd Suits 9⁰⁰

This is a genuine fancy worsted suit, medium heavy weight, and a new pattern for the Fall and Winter season. We contracted for this lot many months ago, and have had thousands of suits made. The fabric is a very strong, firm worsted, having great tenacity of weave. There are several patterns, all similar, medium dark g mixed with either a very fine invisible overplaid or a subdued stripe. The ground is black, which is relieved by the line mixture and indefinite pattern, giving a medium dark affect, just right for general purposes. Coats are made up with genuine haircloth shape-retaining fronts, and mohair serge body lining. All garments are nicely tailored and made to fit. These suits retail generally for from $12.50 to $15.00. They would certainly be very cheap at $10.00, but we are going to see how many thousand we can sell at $9.00. Send order at once, to avoid any chance of delay and disappointment. Men's round sack style.

WE 42 Above described fancy worsted suit. Weight about 6 lbs................................. $9.00

Dry Goods that are Selling Fast—All Bargains

These few dry goods items will fitly illustrate the uniformly good values of our offerings this year. Every section of this popular division is brimming over with just such excellent bargains, and while these are some of the things that others are freely buying, your dry goods wants, whatever they may be, can undoubtedly be supplied from our mammoth collection with the best results possible. Look over the following numbers; they are well worth your attention — every item is a money saver.

Danish Cloth, 12½c

One of the Most Popular of the New Fabrics.

ZE 206. Danish Cloth, 28 inches wide. The popular, inexpensive dress stuff that is advertised so much and selling so fast that the manufacturers are unable to keep up with the demand. We have stocked up on all colors, and have made our price especially low one this season. Half wool and half cotton; looks like wool rep or poplin. Makes up finely for women's or girls' dresses or small boys' suits; washes beautifully and does not shrink. Colors are: Cream, light blue, old rose, tan, gray, cardinal, navy, ron or black. Weight per yard 8 ozs.
Per yard
Full piece of about 60 yds, 12c per yd. **12½c**

50c Melrose Suiting, 39c

Looks as well as Dollar Goods.

ZE 212. A soft, fine, beautiful appearing cloth — the pretty melrose weave that makes up so effectively. It is not an all wool cloth, some fine cotton threads are interwoven, which strengthen but are not seen at all. At a dollar a yard it could look no nicer; at 39 cents it should prove one of our most popular dress goods numbers this year. Colors: Brown, wine, navy, dark green, gray, cardinal, bright blue, cream or black. Width 36 ins. Weight per yard, 4 ounces.
Per yard **39c**

Special Value Black Dress Silks

36-inch Peau de Soie, $1.50.

ZE 110. A new quality this season and extra fine value. Part of a special purchase of black dress silks that we are advertising now. Peau de Soie is the favorite weave for dress skirts or full costumes, and the yard wide goods are popular because they cut to good advantage. This is a soft, rich silk, with beautiful luster and wears exceedingly well. Width 36 ins. Weight per yard 6 ozs. Per yard **$1.50**

Best Quality All Wool Ladies' Cloth, 45c

A Saving of 20 Per Cent.

ZE 216. A specially low price for this mammoth seller this year. There are some poor all wool cloths on the market, but this is not one of them; this is the grade that smaller stores charge 60c for. The most staple winter dress stuff there is: nothing better for warmth and long service; a good bargain. Colors: Light gray mixture, dark gray mixture, tan mixture, cardinal, wine, dark green, light navy, dark navy, dark tan, medium brown, castor, light gray or black. Width 50 inches. Weight per yard 7 ozs. Per yard **45c**

50-in. Mohair Sicilian, 50c

An Exceptional Bargain.

ZE 218. One of the best bargains ever offered in mohair dress goods, and mohairs are having a great run this year. It is a heavier cloth than brilliantine, so well adapted for this time of year, especially in the dark colors that we are listing. Considering the width of it, the value of this staple and very popular dress stuff is unusually good. Colors: Brown, dark green, navy or black. Width 50 inches. Weight per yard 6 ozs. Per yard **50c**

40c All Wool Moreen Skirting, 25c

Regular 40c Quality.

ZE 402. Just one color of this famous petticoat stuff, black only. Everyone knows what moreen is — the rather stiff, watered fabric that usually sells 'round about 40c per yard. We bought this at a bargain, which accounts for our wonderfully low price. Splendid wearing stuff, all wool, but you can buy it here now at the price of a cotton fabric. Width 25 inches. Weight per yard 7 ozs. Per yard **25c**

Good Melton Skirting 25c

Another Popular Bargain

ZE 228. Another of our very popular dress goods numbers, and there is good reason for it — it's remarkably fine value. A new quality this year, rather lighter than last year's cloth; the correct weight for this season, of similar appearance to the dollar goods and makes up about as well. Cotton threads are interwoven which strengthen the fabric but do not show on the face of the cloth. The very best thing going in moderate priced goods. Colors: Medium gray mixture, dark gray mixture, dark blue mixture, plain navy or plain black. Width 29 ins. Weight per yard 7 ozs.
Per yard **25c**

Another Good Silk Bargain

ZE 124. A special purchase of black Brocaded Silks that we are selling for about half the regular price. Taffeta ground with satin fig ures, medium or large, first-class styles; scrolls, flowers and all sorts of good designs, suitable for either waists, skirts or full dresses. We never offered such silk for less than 65c before, and retailers have asked as high as 75c for the same goods. Width 19 ins. Mailing weight per yard 2 ozs. Per yard **39c**

Our Famous German Table Linens

Wonderful Values.

We make a specialty of the soft German and Austrian linens. The specimen numbers quoted below will furnish a good idea of our fine offerings this season.

German Silver Bleached All Linen Table Cloths

A new importation and very good value in moderate priced goods; a splendid, heavy quality of damask drill in new designs; floral, snowdrop, etc. Pure flax all the way through, no stiffening or dressing, will improve in the laundry and soon become snow white. In three sizes.

ZE 561. Size 68x68 inches. Weight 24 ozs. Each **$1.75**

ZE 562. Size 68x88 inches. Weight 29 ozs. Each **2.25**

ZE 563. Size 68x106 inches. Weight 34 ozs. Each **2.75**

Napkins to Match

ZE564. German Silver Bleached All Linen Napkins, matching in quality and design the cloths quoted above. Size 22x22 inches. Weight 28 ozs. Per dozen **$2.00**

Irish Table Damask

A Hummer for $1.00.

Our dollar snow white table damask is a beauty this year, heavy as a board, yet fine, the woven designs showing up with splendid effect; a new quality, and the handsomest we have had for a very long time. ZE595. Fine Snow White Double Satin Damask, 72 inches wide, in beautiful floral or snow drop designs; something especially good for the money. Weight per yard 10 ozs. Per yard **$1.00**

Napkins to Match

ZE 598. Fine Snow White Double Satin Damask Napkins, matching in quality and design ZE595 damask. Size 24x24 ins. Weight 28 ozs. Per dozen **$3.50**

All Wool White Saxony Flannel

50c Value for 37c.

This specimen from our flannel section should clearly demonstrate that our values are far beyond the competition of ordinary stores. A strictly all wool flannel and usually retails at from 45 to 50c per yard. Give us an opportunity of saving you some money on flannels this year.

ZE 704. White All Wool Saxony Flannel, 27 inches wide. Weight per yard 3 ozs. Per yard **37c**

Great Bargains in Blankets and Bedspreads

This section is full of life just now and the good things we have gathered together are beginning to scatter in all directions; wherever they go, one thing we feel sure of—good results, for that was what we thought of more than anything else while selecting the goods. The following are good specimens of our high standard of value this year.

Silver Gray All Wool Blankets

ZE 784. Silver Gray Bed Blankets, strictly all wool. A splendid, stocky, soft and well finished blanket that retailers would ask $4.50 a pair for—something you will like when you get it. Size 60x76 inches. Weight 4 lbs. With fancy striped borders. Per pair **$3.25**

ZE 786. Silver Gray All Wool Bed Blankets, the same quality exactly as ZE784, but larger and heavier. Size 60x80 inches. Weight 5 lbs. Fancy striped borders. $5.50 to $6.00 at retail. Per pair **$4.25**

Fringed Quilts with Cut Corners

ZE 880. A splendid value in White Crochet Quilts; the cut corner style so popular now for brass and iron bedsteads. Has a 5-in. heavy knotted fringe and drapes perfectly 'round the end posts. A heavy, large size quilt with handsome woven designs. Would be good value at $2.00. Size, including fringe, 82x98 in. Weight 3¼ lbs. Each **$1.60**

ZE 686. Handsome White Satin Embroidered Bedspread; bright satin ground with raised embroidered center design and border—a sightly article. Corners are cut out to allow for end posts of bedstead, and it has heavy knotted fringe all around. A beautiful quilt that retailers would charge $4.50 for. Size, not including fringe, 80x90 ins. Weight 4½ lbs. Each **$3.50**

The Damascus Roller Bearing Sewing Machine

LE 78 Mounted on this beautiful $2175 Hand Carved, Piano Polished Automatic Cabinet.

2175

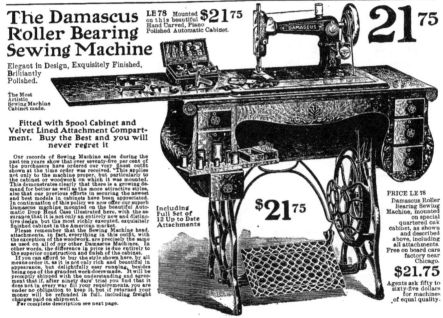

Elegant in Design, Exquisitely Finished, Brilliantly Polished.

The Most Artistic Sewing Machine Cabinet made.

Fitted with Spool Cabinet and Velvet Lined Attachment Compartment. Buy the Best and you will never regret it

Our records of Sewing Machine sales during the past ten years show that over seventy-five per cent of the purchasers have ordered our very finest outfit shown at the time order was received. This applies not only to the machine proper, but particularly to the cabinet or woodwork on which it was mounted. This demonstrates clearly that there is a growing demand for better as well as the more attractive styles, also that our previous efforts in securing the newest and best models in cabinets have been appreciated. In continuation of this policy we now offer our superb Damascus machine mounted on the beautiful Automatic Drop Head Case illustrated here, with the assurance that it is not only an entirely new and distinctive design but the most richly executed, exquisitely finished cabinet in the American market.

Please remember that the Sewing Machine head, attachments, in fact, everything in this outfit, with the exception of the woodwork, are precisely the same as used on all of our other Damascus Machines. In other words, the difference in price is due entirely to the superior construction and finish of the cabinet. If you can afford to buy the style shown here, by all means order it, as it is not only rich and beautiful in appearance, but delightfully easy running, besides being one of the grandest work-doers made. It will be promptly shipped with the understanding and agreement that if, after ninety days' trial you find that it does not in every way fill your requirements, you are under no obligation to keep it, but if returned your money will be refunded in full, including freight charges paid on shipment.

For complete description see next page.

Including Full Set of 12 Up to Date Attachments

$2175

PRICE LE 78 Damascus Roller Bearing Sewing Machine, mounted on special quartered oak cabinet, as shown and described above, including all attachments. Free on board cars factory near Chicago.

$21.75

Agents ask fifty to sixty-five dollars for machines of equal quality.

21⁷⁵ Damascus Roller Bearing Sewing Machine 21⁷⁵

No. LE 78 See illustration on preceding page **Isn't It a Beauty?**

Description of Damascus Sewing Machine LE 78

The top section or table, also the folding leaf, are substantially made on the laminated or built up cross section principle with the different pieces of solid wood glued together so that the grain of one piece runs in the opposite direction to the one next to it, which makes it very durable, besides prevents warping. These sections are then double veneered with selected and beautifully figured quarter sawed oak veneers finished in a rich dark golden color and given the highest piano polish. The ends of table are neatly rounded and finished in a pretty scroll pattern.

THE DRAWER FRAMES as shown in cut are strongly made of an entirely new and graceful style with richly hand carved fronts; there is also a carved ornament in center of front section.

THE DRAWERS, six in number, are of square shape, well made and fitted with fancy metal pulls.

THE DRAWER FRONTS. Sides and fronts of drawer frames are also double veneered in rich quartered oak, and highly polished.

THE SPOOL CABINET. One of the novel as well as desirable features of this new machine is the spool cabinet, which is fitted in one of the drawers. It is supplied with several spindles for holding the different sizes of thread and silk, also has a cushion for the needles, etc. This section is covered with velvet, has a wood handle by which it may be lifted out or returned when necessary.

THE HEAD is our highest grade Damascus, equal or superior in every way to any machine ever built. Taken all in all we consider we have in this combination the most beautiful, the easiest running and highest grade workdoer in the market to-day.

THE ATTACHMENTS. This machine, like all other styles of Damascus, has a complete set of the highest grade nickel plated steel foot attachments, as follows: Ruffler or Gatherer, Tucker, Narrow Feller, four Hemmers, assorted widths, Binder, Braider, Quilter and Shirring Plate. It is also supplied with the regular accessories, such as twelve Needles, six Bobbins, two Screw Drivers and Oil Can filled with Oil. These attachments are placed in one of the drawers which is specially fitted up for them with racks, etc., and is lined throughout with velvet.

AUTOMATIC LIFT. This cabinet has our latest automatic lifting device which works easily and accurately, besides is very simple and durable.

THE STAND is the broad ribbon pattern, light and graceful, at the same time strong and lasting.

ROLLER BEARINGS. As a matter of course this grand machine is equipped with our new special easy running devices, ROLLER BEARINGS AND STEEL BALL AND SOCKET PITMAN, beyond question the greatest improvement ever made in developing the easy running features of the sewing machine.

Ninety Days' Trial

Remember, that in ordering any one of our sewing machines, it is shipped with the understanding and agreement that the deal is not to be considered closed until ninety days after it arrives in your own home IN GOOD ORDER. This gives you a splendid opportunity to test every feature, including the attachments. If you wish to order any other machine for comparison, you have ample time to do so. If our machine does not please you in every way, we do not want you to keep it.

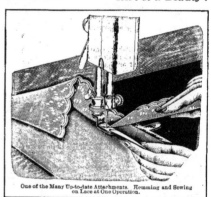

One of the Many Up-to-date Attachments. Hemming and Sewing on Lace at One Operation.

Price, LE 78 Roller Bearing Sewing Machine—Mounted on special quartered oak cabinet as shown and described on opposite page, including all attachments. Free on board cars factory (near Chicago)............................ **$21.75**
Shipping weight, 120 lbs.

Bargains for the Beginner and Amateur

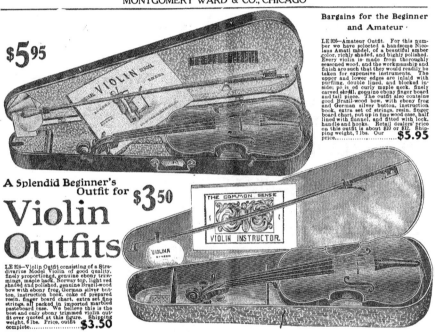

$5⁹⁵

LE 326—Amateur Outfit. For this number we have selected a handsome Nicolaus Amati model, of a beautiful amber color, richly shaded, and highly polished. Every violin is made from thoroughly seasoned wood, and the workmanship and finish are such that they would readily be taken for expensive instruments. The upper and lower edges are inlaid with purfling, double lined, and blocked inside; po is ed or curly maple neck, finely carved scroll, genuine ebony finger board and tail piece. The outfit also contains good Brazil-wood bow, with ebony frog and German silver button, instruction book, extra set of strings, resin, finger board chart, put up in fine wood case, half lined with flannel, and fitted with lock, handle and hooks. Retail dealers' price on this outfit is about $10 or $12. Shipping weight, 7 lbs. Our price....................**$5.95**

A Splendid Beginner's Outfit for **$3**⁵⁰

Violin Outfits

LE 324—Violin Outfit consisting of a Stradivarius Model Violin of good quality, finely proportioned, genuine ebony trimmings, maple back, Norway top, light red shaded and polished, genuine Brazil-wood bow with ebony frog, German silver button, instruction book, cake of prepared resin, finger board chart, extra set fine strings, all packed in imported marbled pasteboard case. We believe this is the best and only ebony trimmed violin outfit ever quoted at this figure. Shipping weight, 6 lbs. Price, outfit complete....................**$3.50**

A Beautiful Design 2⁷⁵
The Victoria Dinner Set—Thirty Pieces
30 Pieces

Will Stand Hard Use

We have made this set up for small families or those needing only a small set. Every piece in the assortment is useful. The ware is cream white, decorated with bright pink flowers and buds arranged in sprays with green leaves and stems. The edges and handles are trimmed with gold. To anyone desiring a useful small dinner set that will stand everyday wear, we heartily recommend this one.

Thirty pieces decorated dinner ware for................. $2⁷⁵

Thirty Pieces—Enough for Small Families

6 Tea Cups
6 Tea Saucers
6 Plates, actual measure, 7¼ in.

6 Plates, actual measure, 9¼ in.
1 Platter, 11¼ in. actual measure
1 Oval Open Vegetable Dish

1 Round Open Vegetable Dish
1 Covered Sugar Bowl (2 pieces)
1 Cream Pitcher

BE 34 The Victoria Dinner Set, packed for shipment by freight. Weight, packed, 50 lbs. We have purchased a large quantity and offer them in the above 30-piece assortment only at the extremely low price of, per set..

2⁷⁵
30 Pieces

Accordions

At about Half Dealers' Prices

Instruction Book Free

Weidlich's Empress Accordion $1 95

Zimmerman's Patent Autoharp

Although the autoharp has been on the market for many years, it is still one of the most popular instruments of its kind made; as a matter of fact, our sales during the past year have nearly doubled. The reason for this is, it is a musical instrument possessing a splendid quality of tone and so simple in construction and manner of operation that any person, or even a child, can produce perfect chords, either as an accompaniment to the voice in singing or with any other instrument, without any knowledge whatever of music. Besides, anyone capable of singing a tune correctly can with little practice play instrumental pieces with marvelous effect. They are made of seasoned materials, have a perfect sounding board, and are finely finished. Send us your order for one and if after a trial of 10 days you are not satisfied, return it at our expense both ways and we will refund your money. The patent attachment, consisting of 6 bars, is placed directly over the strings and is so constructed that when either bar is pressed down only the strings needed for the

The Celebrated Pitzschler at $5 00

chord are left free to vibrate, all the others being stopped or deadened. Thus when the pick is drawn across the strings perfect harmony is produced. Instruction book containing 13 pieces of music, tuning wrench and picks furnished with each instrument.
LE 307 Autoharp No. 2½; ebonized case with yellow sounding board, highly varnished; has 23 strings, 6 bars producing 5 chords in key of C; size 18x10; well finished throughout. Shipping weight, 5 lbs. Retail price, $5.00 our price:

$5.50 Autoharp for $2 95

This is one of the sweetest toned instruments you ever heard, and so simple that anyone can easily learn to play.

LE 267 Weidlich's Empress Accordion, imitation mahogany case, size 10x6, with raised mouldings, open action, 10 nickel-plated valve keys, 2 sets of reeds, 2 stops, 2 basses, double bellows, full nickel trimmings. The best and only accordion made by a responsible manufacturer that we have ever been able to offer at this price. Shipping weight, 7 lbs. Each...................$1.95

LE 292 Pitzschler Accordion of handsome model, polished ebonized mouldings with outer edge neatly decorated, top panel elaborately ornamented with pearl designs, open key-board, 10 fancy keys, pearl buttons, 2 sets reeds, 2 stops, 2 basses, 2 double bellows, sides neatly finished with nickel bands and protectors. One of the finest double reed accordions made. Size, 13x7. Shipping weight, about 10 lbs. Each..**$5.00**

Please compare this line with any similar line of leather top rubber overshoes, and note the superiority of the materials in our shoe. From the Kangaroo calf-skin in the tops to the stitching in the vamps, everything is of the best. The tops are made from pliable Kangaroo calf and can be used over and over again after the rubbers are worn out, and they remain perfectly soft without greasing after being wet. The rubber overshoes are best quality duck, made by a reliable manufacturer, and are as near crackproof as it is possible to make them. Nothing better obtainable and worth at least $2.50 per pair. Height from heel to top, 10 inches. Wide widths only. Weight, 36 to 48 ounces, according to size.

UE 432 Boys' sizes, 1 to 5. Per pair $1.48. UE 431 Men's sizes 6 to 12. Per pair.... **$1 90**

Leather top Rubber Overshoes $1.90

The Kant-Rip shoe for men is the best work shoe ever devised. We call them the Kant-Rip shoe because there is nothing about them to rip, being as near seamless as it is possible to make them, the only seams being at the top and back where there is little or no wear. The lower seam shown in illustration is only an imitation. They are made from soft, durable, water-shedding oil grain leather with heavy rugged soles firmly riveted to the uppers. They are made on a stylish last, fit fine, wear like iron and make a very neat and genteel appearance. Shoes like these are seldom sold for less than $2.50 per pair, but as usual our price is way down. Weight, 36 to 48 ounces, according to size. Wide widths only. Sizes 5 to 12. Per pair........$1.55

Order UE 898.

Seamless "Kant-Rip" Shoe

Sold everywhere for $2.50 **$1 55**

Boys' Ruff-and-Tumble Shoes $1.25—98c

Here we offer you a line of boys' shoes that gives you three things in one, what you want in shoes but seldom get —good looks, hard service and low prices, made from extra prime selected satin calf stock with strong rugged soles. The shape is a neat appearing, easy fitting round toe which will give comfort to the wearer. We have handled this line for years with splendid satisfaction, and we unhesitatingly say they are worth at least a third more than we ask for them. Weight, 18 to 36 ounces, according to size. Wide widths only.

UE 146 Sizes, 9 to 13½. Per pair.... **98c**

UE 150 Sizes, 1 to 5½. Per pair. **$1.25**

Women's Stylish Fall Footwear $1.35

These shoes are superior in style and wearing qualities to most footwear at this price, and we do not brag when we say that they are equal to many similar lines sold elsewhere at $2.50 or even $3.00 per pair. They are made from fine Vici kid, known as the best leather for women's shoes. The shape is stylish and comfortable and assures the wearer a neat appearing, easy fitting shoe. The soles are not too heavy for comfort, yet heavy enough to give splendid service. Fancy velvet lace stay. Weight, 16 to 24 ounces, according to size. Wide widths only. Order UE 50. Sizes 2½ to 8. Per pair....................$1.35

Ladies' Felt Juliets

85c

Startling value. Actually worth $1.50. Of course, there are any number of cheap juliets on the market, but ours are cheap only in price. They are made by the Dolgeville Felt Shoe Co., Dolgeville, New York, whose slippers are looked upon by the trade as the top notch of excellence. The felt and fur used and the flexible belting leather in the soles are the best and form a happy combination for comfort, warmth and durability. Slippers like these are sold everywhere at $1.25 to $1.50 per pair. Weight, 16 to 20 ounces. Wide widths only. Sizes 2½ to 9. Order No. UE 96.

Price, per pair.. **85c**

A Bargain for Baby

One of the best bargains we have ever offered our customers. Stylish patent leather shoes, fancy stitched, with pink, white and blue kid tops. The whole outfit is novel, pretty, and the assortment of colors to match dresses of similar color makes it very practicable. These shoes are packed three pairs to the box. Sizes as you want them and are sold singly at 40c per pair or three pairs for 75c. Sizes 1 to 4. Weight, 4 ounces.
UE 103. One pair, 40c. UE 109. Three pairs **75c**

Infants' Durable Shoes

48c

These shoes are fine for infants who require footwear that will stand hard knocks.

The upper leather is Vici kid, soft and durable, and the soles are white oak, hand turned, flexible and durable. The shape is a broad and roomy one, allowing plenty of room for the toes to grow. We consider these shoes worth at least 75c per pair. Weight, 6 to 8 ounces, according to sizes. Wide widths only.

UE 238 Infants'. Sizes 2 to 5. No heel. Per pair............ **48c**

UE 232 Child's. Sizes 4 to 8. Spring heel. Per pair **75c**

Arctic Over-shoes

$1.10

You run no risk in buying these articles for there is nothing better made. They are warm, durable, comfortable and water proof, and are priced very low. First quality only. Every pair guaranteed.

UE 376.	Men's, sizes 6 to 13, per pair......	**$1.10**
UE 378.	Women's, sizes 2½ to 9, per pair...	**80c**
UE 383.	Girls', sizes 11 to 2, per pair......	**64c**
UE 395.	Child's, sizes 5 to 10½, per pair...	**52c**
UE 403.	Boys', sizes 3 to 6, per pair......	**93c**
UE 404.	Boys', sizes 10 to 2, per pair......	**74c**

48c

Girls' Rough and Ready Shoes

Little money buys good shoes now-a-days, which you will admit when you see the goods. These shoes are made from soft, durable Kangaroo Grain leather with rugged soles, firmly riveted to the uppers. The soles, insoles and counters are solid leather and will give splendid service. These shoes can't rip, because there is nothing about them to rip, being practically seamless, the only seams being at the top and inside of the shoes where there is little or no wear. Weight, 14 to 20 ounces, according to sizes. Wide widths only.

UE 1200 Sizes 13 to 2. Per pair.... **90c**

UE 1201 Sizes 8 to 12. Per pair.... **80c**

Shoe, Harness and Tinware Repair Set

A High-grade Set of Tools at Rock Bottom Price

$1.48

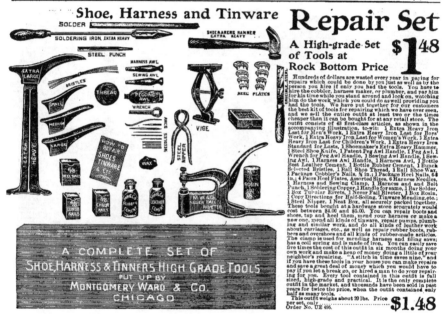

Hundreds of dollars are wasted every year in paying for repairs which could be done by you just as well as by the person you hire if only you had the tools. You have to hire the cobbler, harness maker, or plumber, and pay him for his time while you stand around and look on, watching him do the work which you could do as well providing you had the tools. We have put together for our customers the best kit of tools for repairing which we have ever seen, and we sell the entire outfit at least two or the times cheaper than it can be bought for at any retail store. The outfit consists of 43 first-class articles, as shown in the accompanying illustration, to-wit: 1 Extra Heavy Iron Last for Men's Work, 1 Extra Heavy Iron Last for Boys' Work, 1 Extra Heavy Iron Last for Women's Work. 1 Extra Heavy Iron Last for Children's Work, 1 Extra Heavy Iron Standard for Lasts, 1 Shoemaker's Extra Heavy Hammer, 1 Steel Shoe Knife, 1 Patent Peg Awl Handle, 1 Peg awl, 1 Wrench for Peg Awl Handle, 1 Sewing Awl Handle, 1 Sewing Awl, 1 Harness Awl Handle, 1 Harness Awl, 1 Bottle Best Leather Cement, 1 Bottle Rubber Cement, 1 Bunch Selected Bristles, 1 Ball Shoe Thread, 1 Ball Shoe Wax, 1 Package Cobbler's Nails, ⅝ in.1 Package Heel Nails, 6⅛ in.1 4 Pairs Heel Plates, Assorted Sizes, 6 Harness Needles, 1 Harness and Sewing Clamp, 1 Harness and and Belt Punch, 1 Soldering Copper,1 Handle for same, 1 Bar Solder, 1 Box Tubular Rivets, 1 Never Fail Riveter, 1 Box Rosin, 1 Copy Directions for Half-Soling, Tinware Mending, etc.; 1 Steel Nipper, 1 Neat Box, all securely packed together. These tools bought at a hardware store separately would cost between $4.00 and $5.00. You can repair boots and shoes, tap and heel them, mend your harness or make a new one, mend all kinds of tinware, repair pumps, plumbing and similar work, and do all kinds of leather work about carriages, etc., as well as repair rubber boots, rubbers and overshoes and all kinds of rubber-made articles. The clamp is used for mending harness and filing saws; has a coil spring and is made of iron. You can easily save five times the cost of this outfit in six months doing your own work and make a heap of money doing a little of your neighbor's repairing. "A stitch in time saves nine," and if you have these tools in your house you can make repairs and save a great deal of money which you would have to pay if you let a break go, or hired a man to do your repairing for you. Every tool contained in this outfit is full sized, high-grade and practical. It is the only complete outfit in the market, and thousands have been sold in past years for twice the price, when the outfit contained only half as many tools.

This outfit weighs about 20 lbs. Price per set, only **$1.48**
Order No. UE 496.

Guard Your Health

Every family should have always on hand a few simple, efficient remedies as a safeguard against the ills to which mankind is heir.

"A stitch in time saves nine."

The M. W. & Co. Home Remedy Set

Order **GE 25**

$2 48

Costs no more than a single visit of the doctor, and it will save many visits and prevent the loss of time and unpleasantness of the sickness itself.

Weight, 16 lbs.

The Set Consists of

Medicine Cabinet—Well made of solid oak, and finished golden. Size, 22x14 in. Inside is partitioned for different size bottles.

Pilgrim's Blood and Iron Pills—This pill is just such an article as people want who are run down and wish something to build up the system; it makes rich, red blood. One box.

Compound Extract Sarsaparilla—A valuable blood purifier and system regulator. One bottle.

Pilgrim's Diarrhoea Cordial—An article of immense sale, from an old and tried prescription, and the best diarrhoea remedy that can be found. One bottle.

Fig Laxative—A pleasant, safe and non-gripping laxative medicine; one that will cure constipation and not ruin the stomach. One bottle.

M. W. & Co.'s Cough Syrup—An old and well known preparation for relieving and curing all forms of colds. It always gives satisfaction. One bottle.

Quinine Pills—Montgomery Ward & Co.'s sulphate quinine pills, 2-grain, gelatine-coated, 100 in bottle. One bottle.

Little Liver Pills—Forty small but very active little pills in a glass vial, with circular in English and German. One bottle.

Seidlitz Powders.—Pure, full strength, in tin boxes, 10 powders in a box.

"Thornward" Borated Talcum Powder—Put up in our own laboratory, and we guarantee it equal to the very best. The most soothing preparation for the skin made. Put up in neat tin boxes. One box.

You Cannot Afford to be Without This Remedy Set. Order Today.

Drugs and Patent Medicines

We Save You From 20 to 25 Per Cent on Patent Medicines and From 20 to 40 Per Cent on Drugs.

Why Not Look Ahead and Lay in a Supply of Such Articles as Are Always Needed.

We call your attention to a few items taken from the Drug Section of our General Catalogue No. 73, which we are sure will interest you. If you are in need of anything in this line not quoted by us write for our quotations, as we can supply you at prices far below those usually charged in retail drug stores.

	Reg. Price.	Our Price.	Per Doz.
GE 180—Peruna	$1.00	.70	$8.00
GE 800—Liquozone, large	1.00	.75	8.50
GE 100—Pierce's Favorite Prescription	1.00	.70	8.00
GE 110—Pierce's Golden Medical Discovery	1.00	.70	8.00
GE 013—Pierce's Purgative Pellets	.25	.15	1.00
GE 596—Castoria (Genuine)	.35	.24	2.90
GE 329—Shoop's Restorative	1.00	.75	8.50
GE 746—Mellin's Infant Food	.75	.50	6.50
GE 964—Sulphur Flour, 175 and 250 lbs.		3c lb.	
	Sulphur Flour, 100 lb. bags	3½c lb.	
GE 229—Copperas, bble 420 to 450 lbs.		1c lb	
	Copperas, 50 lbs. to 100 lbs.	2c lb	
GE 280—Dist. Extract Witch Hazel, best quality, per gallon jug		95c	
GE 13—Crude Carbolic Acid, per gallon can		57c	

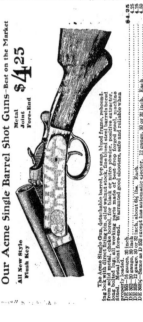

Buy them now

Don't wait until the winter is half over and miss much of the joy in their use. You will need some of the popular offerings on this page. They are all of reliable grade and will please you.

Boys' and Men's Skates.

DE 660—This skate runner is made from the best rolled cast steel plates. The clamps, etc., of cold rolled steel, bright finish. The runners are highly polished. It can be adjusted to fit a large or small boot heel. Always give size of skate wanted in inches when ordering; sizes 8 to 12 in. Per pair **46c**

Children's Skates.

DE 662—Children's Extension Bob Skate, especially for small children learning to skate. The runners are wide apart and there is no danger of straining the ankles. Extends from 6 to 9 inches. Per pair.......... **40c**

Ladies' Ice Skates.

DE 584—Ladies' Club Skate, with rolled cast steel polished runners, bright steel toe and heel plates. Russian leather straps. Sizes; 8½, 9, 9½, 10, 10½. Always gives sizes in inches when ordering. Per pair **75c**

Striking Bags.

DE 175—The Frazier Patent Bag, lightest and fastest made; it has no lacing, thus doing away with the unpleasant feature of inflating the ordinary bag; the loop being attached to an inner washer removes the strain from the sides, as in the ordinary bag; it is made of the best selected oil-tanned horse hide, thoroughly stretched, is hand sewed with welt seams; best bag on the market.
Each.................... **$2.50**

DE 178—M. W. & Co.'s "Practice" Single Loop Striking Bag, made of fine grain colored leather, colored top and bottom, well sewed, drill lined, complete with bladder, rope and screw eye; regulation size. 30 in. circumference Each **$1.00**

Smokers' Articles.

DE 888—Finest quality Vienna Meerschaum, boiled in wax, so it will color same as genuine Meerschaum. Eagle claw bowl. Nicely carved, with Weichsel stem 6 inches long. Imitation amber mouthpiece. Silk tassels. Length over all about 10 inches. Each.......... **$1.00**

DE 901—Finest French Brier, oval shape bowl, silver band on bowl, genuine amber mouth piece, 2½ in. long; a good size bowl, with a fine vestpocket style, leather covered, velvet lined case. This is one of the latest designs with bent stem, and a fine and very desirable pipe; entire length about 5 in. Each.......... **$1.85**

DE 854—Same style and general description as DS858, except 5 in. high and 3¾ in. base. Weight 16 oz. Each.......... **50c**

DE 353.   DE 901.

DE 353—Cigar or Tobacco Jar. Fancy imitation cut glass, poppy design, nicely finished and embossed. Oxidized finished cover, with place to insert a damp sponge, making a neat and useful article. Just the thing for keeping your cigars and tobacco nice and fresh; 6½ in. high, 6 in. wide across base. Weight 40 oz. Each.................. **$1.00**

DE 357 Cigar or Tobacco Jar. Fancy imitation cut glass, bulb shape; nicely finished and embossed, cupid design; metal cover, gold or silver finish, making a neat appearing and useful article. Will keep cigars and tobacco fresh and moist, which is relished by every smoker; height 9 in.; width across 5⅜ in.; weight 40 oz.
Each.................. **75c**

Boxing Gloves.

DE 151—Corbett Pattern Boxing Glove, tan color, leather padded lace wrist, serge lined, well made, and a good glove. 6 oz. Per set of 4 gloves **2.50**

Amateur or Practice Foot Balls.

DE 974—Practice Foot Ball, made of good strong leather. Rugby shape complete with bladder. This ball is made good and strong, and will give good satisfaction. Regulation size, 27 in. Postage 15 cents extra.
Each.................... **90c**

DE 977—Amateur Association Foot Ball, made of good strong leather, complete with bladder; well made, good quality. 27 in. ball. Postage 15 cents extra.
Each.......... **$1.00**

Torchon Trimming
Very Durable for Underwear

We offer here a few numbers of our popular Torchon Insertion and Edging to match. The patterns are new this season, being imported by us direct from the world's most famous fashion centers. You will not find such dainty patterns, desirable qualities and low prices elsewhere.

SE 254—Extra fine quality white English Torchon lace edging.

Width.	Per yard.	Per doz.
1¼ in.	5c	50c
2 in.	6c	60c
3¼ in.	8c	75c

SE 251—Extra fine quality white English Torchon lace insertion; width 1½ in. Per yard....**5c** Per doz.............50c

SE 249—Special value in white English Torchon edge; width, 1¼ in. Per yard.........**3c** Per doz.........30c

SE 247—Special value in white English Torchon insertion; width 1¼ in. Per yard.........**3c** Per doz.........30c

Cambric Insertion

SE 017—Cambric Insertion, embroidery 1 in.; full width. 2 in. Per yard...**8c**

SE 841—Cambric Embroidery; 3 dainty patterns, ⅜-in. work, full width, 1¼ in. Per yard....**5c**

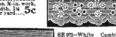

SE 971—White Cambric Insertion; width, 2 in.; embroidered 1¼ in. Per yard..........**9c**

SE 973—Edging to match, 4 in. wide, embroidered, 1¼ in. deep. Per yard..........**10c**

SE 977—White Cambric Embroidered Edge, 3½ in. deep; 7½ in. wide. Per yard....**18c**

SE 979—Wide Edging to match; 10 in. wide, embroidered 4½ in. deep. Per yard....**25c**

SE 971 to 979

Bargains
For the Dressing Table
Toilet and Sewing Rooms

SE 507—Large Cube containing 100 best steel pins with glass heads; assorted black and colors. This is the very best cube to be obtained at the usual 10c price. It makes a very showy ornament as well as a convenient article. Price, each..........**5c**

SE 597—Cabinet of 200 assorted black wire hairpins, from the finest crimp lace to the large straight or crimpled hair pin used for the back hair. All sizes and styles; almost anything that can be asked for in this kind of hair pin, and the quality is such are nicely put up in different compartments in a neat plaid cabinet. Per box............**5c**

Ladies' Work Box, 25c

SE 602—Work Box, 6x3½ in., 1¼ in. high, containing a good supply of Thos. Harper & Sons' gold-eyed sewing needles, rug, crewel and chenille needles. It is also supplied with darning, tape, and crochet needles and two spools darning cotton —black and white. Handsomely embossed cover. Price, each...**25c**

Looks Like Silk

The new, beautiful mercerized crochet cotton in wash colors. One of the newest things on the market and selling by the box like wildfire. Per spool......... **2½c**

Mer-Kot-Silk
For Crocheting, Knitting and Embroidery

SE 894—Mer-Kot-Silk, made of cotton, 82 yards on spool, a new production made to imitate silk, at a much lower price; permanent luster; plain wash colors, as follows: White, rose pink, light pink, scarlet, sky blue, light blue, marine, navy, yellow, orange, nile green, moss green, myrtle green, grass green, lilac, fast dark red; fast black, heliotrope, purple, cerise, golden brown or medium brown. Weight per box 14 oz. Per 10 spools.....................24c Per spool **2½c**

SE 895—Mer-Kot-Silk, same as above, in combination colors as follows: White and yellows, white and blues, white and pinks, white and nile greens, white and moss greens, white and lilacs, white, yellow and burnt orange, white, blue and pink, white, yellow and pink, white, green and pink, white, green and yellow, red, white and blue. Per 10 spools...24c Per spool.................................**2½c**

Phenomenal Selling

XE 4–A $7.50
Jacket at

$4.95

We originally bought of these two jackets (XE 4 and XE 8) 10,000 each, thinking that this quantity would be ample to supply those of our customers who might think favorably of these styles, but we had no more than sent out the first edition of our catalogue before the orders began to come in for them so fast that we felt obliged to arrange for another large lot and are pleased to announce that we have succeeded in securing enough Kersey for another lot as large as the first one, and will continue to sell them at the same price, notwithstanding they cost us 50 cts. each extra on account of having to have them made up in the busy season.

XE 60—This coat is made of good quality heavy weight wool Cassimere. Color, dark Oxford gray. Style same as illustrated, coat collar of velvet, belt in back, made very full and is intended to be worn loose, therefore it would be advisable when ordering to order one size larger than is actually required in tight fitting garments. Supplied with patch pockets; unlined. Front has deep facing extending back to arm holes; 46 inches long. Weight, 45 oz.
Each.................. **$5.75**

XE 60

$5.75

SIZES
32
to
42

XE 8
An $8.50
Jacket for

$5.50

XE 4—This swell collarless jacket is made of all-wool Kersey; colors, black or castor; trimmed around the neck with a stitched scalloped band with points extending out over the shoulders representing epaulets; the edges of the stitched band are finished with novelty silk braid, and same braid is used for trimming on cuffs, ornamented with metal buttons; lined with best quality mercerized fabric; 26 inches long, finished around the edges with tailor stitching and supplied with two pockets as shown in illustration. Nothing quite so good as this jacket has ever been offered by us before and we guarantee it to be equal in every respect to jackets sold by retailers throughout the country at $7.50. Weight, 46 oz. Each.................... **$4.95**

XE 8—This attractive jacket is made of good quality all-wool Kersey; colors, black or castor; made with storm collar and trimmed around the neck with stitched velvet as shown in illustration; front and back are trimmed with bands of the material, ornamented with small silk buttons; half tight fitted back; full front, lined with finest quality mercerized serge; 26 inches long. An extraordinary value at price mentioned; we have no doubt but that retailers throughout the country will sell a like garment at $8.50. Weight, 45 oz. Each **$5.50**

Women's Petticoats

Sizes: 39, 40, 41 & 42 in. long

Examine them Critically

Read every description carefully. We positively know these values cannot be duplicated elsewhere.

1 25

XE 626

1 65

XE 620

XE 616

95c

1 45

XE626—This handsome petticoat is made of fine quality mercerized fabric. Style same as illustration; flounce is trimmed with three-inch ruffle of accordion plaiting, edged with two-inch ruffle of the material and has three bands of the material for a heading. A regular $1.60 value. Weight, 17 oz. Each....... **$1.25**

XE616—This skirt is made of a good quality of fast black mercerized fabric. The deep flounce is trimmed with four bands of material and faced with canvas; the upper part of skirt is lined with Domet flannel. A very desirable skirt for Winter wear, especially adapted for elder y women. Weight, 18 oz. Each...**95c**

XE620—This handsome style is made from very fine quality mercerized fabric. The deep umbrella flounce is trimmed with a ruffle of accordion plaiting and fancy stitching and two narrow bands of the material. The upper part of skirt is lined with Domet flannel. It is a very warm and serviceable skirt for Winter wear. Weight, 20 oz. Each................ **$1.65**

XE 612

Waist and Skirt Bargains
We save you fully 1-4 to 1-3 on Stylish, Reliable, Apparel

Women's Waists

98c
XE150

95c
XE114

Regular Sizes { Bust, 32, 34, 36, 38, 40 and 42 inches. Waist, 22, 24, 26, 28, 30 and 32 inches.
{ Length of Sleeve, inside, 18½ inches. Length of Waist, back, 16½ inches.

NOTE—These waists come in regular sizes only. Any orders received with measurements that do not come in accordance with above scale we will be obliged to make to special order for which we will be obliged to make an additional charge of 10 per cent and a delay in filling order of about a week's time. Allowance for both should be made. The waist measurement is always 10 inches less than the bust measure in regular stock sizes.

$5.95
XE422

Women's Walking Skirts

SCALE OF SIZES: Waist Band, 23, 24, 25, 26, 27, 28, 29 and 30 in. Length, 38, 39, 40, 41, 42 and 43 in.

All these styles have an inverted plait in the back.
XE430 This walking skirt is made of printed meltonette, a very serviceable fabric especially suitable for these skirts. The color is a dark gray with stripes of green and cardinal, made like the illustration, lapped seams with double stitching, finished around the bottom with a band of the material, stitched with rows of stitching. We have 16,000 of these skirts for this sale. Nothing quite as good will be found among the **$1.48** retailer's for less than $2.50. Each....

$1.48
XE430

SIZES:
Waist, 23 to 30 inches;
Length, 39 to 43 inch.

$2.75
XE432

XE150 This waist is an exceptional value; it is made from all-wool twilled Flannel; colors are gray, dark cardinal, navy blue or black; style same as illustrated; made with detachable tab collar; unlined and splendidly finished through out; this is the best value we have ever been able to offer in an all-wool waist at this price; in the past seasons the best we have been able to do for a waist at this price was to furnish a plain light-weight flannel; we have no doubt at all but the retailers will get at least $1.35 for no better waist than this one. Weight, 8 oz. Each................. **98c**

XE422 This stylish skirt is made of fine quality novelty all-wool cassimere suiting; colors are royal blue or black ground, with an indistinct broken plaid of gray; style same as illustration; side gores are trimmed with band of material ornamented with small silk buttons and plaiting extending from band down to the bottom, splendidly tailored throughout; a very rich and fashionable skirt; equal in every respect to the $8.50 to $10 skirts sold by retailers. Wt. 28 oz. Ea.. **$5.95**

XE114 This waist is made of a fine quality Mercerized Sateen; color, black; style, same as illustrated; front is embroidered with silk and center-piece is finished with fine tucking and ornamented with small buttons; back is plaited from neck to waist line; unlined; detachable tab collar. An exceptional value. Weight, 8 oz. Each................. **95c**

XE432 This fashionable Walking Skirt is made of fine all-wool Cassimere. Color, dark Oxford gray. Made like the illustration, seams are lapped and double stitched.
On either side of the front gore is an inverted plait extending from waist to bottom, and just below the knee are pointed tabs of the material, finished around the bottom with a band of the material, stitched with rows of stitching, inverted plait in back. The equal of skirts sold at retail for $4.50. Our price....................... **$2.75**

We have 10,000 for this sale. SIZES—Waist band, 23 to 30 in. Length, 39 to 43 in.

Style, Service and Satisfaction.

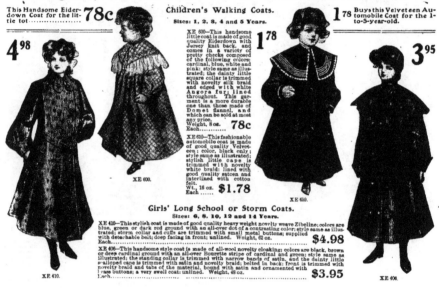

This Handsome Eider-down Coat for the little tot 78c

4⁹⁸

Children's Walking Coats.
Sizes: 1, 2, 3, 4 and 5 Years.

1⁷⁸

Buys this Velveteen Automobile Coat for the 1-to-5-year-old.

3⁹⁵

XE 600—This handsome little coat is made of good quality Eiderdown with Jersey knit back, and comes in a variety of pretty checks composed of the following colors: cardinal, blue, white and pink; style same as illustrated; the dainty little square collar is trimmed with novelty silk braid and edged with white Angora fur; lined throughout. This garment is a more durable one than those made of Domet flannel, and which can be sold at most any price. Weight, 8 oz. Each............ 78c

XE 610—This fashionable automobile coat is made of good quality Velveteen; color, black only; style same as illustrated; stylish little cape is trimmed with novelty white braid; lined with good quality sateen and interlined with cotton felt. Wt., 16 oz. Each...... $1.78

XE 600.

XE 610.

Girls' Long School or Storm Coats.
Sizes: 6, 8, 10, 12 and 14 Years.

XE 410—This stylish coat is made of good quality heavy weight novelty weave Zibeline; colors are blue, green or dark red ground with an all-over dot of a contrasting color; style same as illustrated; storm collar and cuffs are trimmed with small metal buttons; supplied with detachable belt; deep facing in front; unlined. Weight, 62 oz. Each.................. $4.98

XE 406—This handsome style coat is made of all-wool novelty cloaking; colors are black, brown or deep cardinal ground with an all-over Bourette stripe of cardinal and green; style same as illustrated; the standing collar is trimmed with narrow bands of satin, and the dainty little scalloped cape is trimmed with satin and novelty braid; belted in back; front is trimmed with novelty braid and tabs of the material, bound with satin and ornamented with brass buttons; a very swell coat; unlined. Weight, 48 oz. Each................. .... $3.95

XE 410.

XE 406.

Greatest Comfort, Least Expense

$25

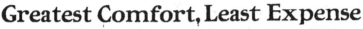

$14⁵⁰   **$11⁵⁰**

Sizes for these coats run as high as 52-inch chest measure. As they are not sized the same as cloth coats we do not give the scale of sizes, for fear they will cause confusion. When ordering give your regular tailor's chest measure. Larger sizes than 52 inches we will be obliged to make special measurements, for which we make an extra charge.

Our Popular Goat Coats.

XE 400 This coat is made of gray goat skin and is a very popular coat with us on account of its extraordinary wearing qualities and moderate price. It is often sold for Norway dog, and is given this fictitious name to mislead, and enable the unscrupulous dealer to get more money for them. It is lined with quilted Italian lining of a very serviceable quality; supplied with leather shields under the arms. We have supplied ourselves with an immense quantity of these coats and will offer them at the same low price as last season. Weight, 11 lbs.
Each **$11.50**

Our Successful Wombat Coat.

XE 444 This coat is made of Australian wombat, a very popular fur because of its warmth, wearing qualities and lightness of weight; we have had a large quantity made up of the brown colors, which are not as desirable as the silver gray, but the wearing qualities and warmth are equal to any; style same as XE 446; lined with best quilted lining and supplied with leather shields under arms. Weight, about 9 pounds.
Each **$14.50**

XE 446 This coat is made of finer quality silver gray wombat. The skins are nicely matched and are of the best quality, being very densely furred, lined with best quilted lining and are equal to similar coats sold at retail for $25.00. Weight, 9 lb.
Each **$21.00**

Fur Lined Coat.

XE 502 This coat is made of all wool Kersey shell and lined with black dog fur and trimmed with sable blended rat collar as shown in illustration; sleeves are lined with long knap Mackinaw cloth, as warm, and looks very much like fur.
Weight, 11 pounds. Each **$25.00**

Our reputation stands back of every Coat.

XE 502   XE 446   XE 400

Safe from the Cold

Our Underwear Protects You

No Shoddy Goods In Our Stock

These lots are all made to order for us and special care used in every part of the manufacture. No job lots, no odds and ends, every garment guaranteed. Men's Underwear for Winter is a special feature with us, and we challenge the world on variety, quality and low prices. We have an exceptionally fine line this year, and the expense will be ours if we cannot satisfy you, as your money will be refunded if we do not please you in every particular.

Extra Special. Our Celebrated Standard $1.00 Under-Wear

TE 332—Montgomery Ward & Co.'s standard One Dollar Undershirt. Natural gray color. Good heavy winter weight. Better value never before offered. One dollar never bought the equal. Made to order for us from selected scoured wool and worsted. The thread is hard spun and twisted before knitting, making a very strong, firm cloth that will shrink very little and will remain soft and pliable. These garments will not irritate the skin. Same quality as last year, and well worth $1.50 at retail. We have made a special effort on this particular garment and feel sure you will recognize the extreme value. Sizes, 34 to 50 in. chest measure. Price per shirt.............. **$1.00**
Price per half dozen..$5.70

TE 334—Montgomery Ward & Co.'s Standard One Dollar Drawers to match TE 332. Same extra fine quality, natural gray color, special finish, double crotch, double stitched seams, and crotch seams reinforced with tape, good heavy winter weight. You get quality, strength and warmth in these—our standard wool garments. Sizes 30 to 50 waist measure. Price per pair.. **$1.00**
Price per half dozen..$5.70

Do not forget to give size wanted

Average weight of either shirt or drawers in winter underwear is one pound per garment.

Men's Fleeced or Plush Back Wool Underwear

The garments under this heading are heavy winter weight, soft wool, and have the special feature of a fleeced lining, which makes them much softer and warmer. The fleecing is made by weaving an extra thread as a backing to the shirt, and then brushing it up to a soft fleece.

Special $1.10

TE 372 Men's Plush or Fleeced Back Undershirts, fine soft wool, heavy weight, golden brown color; something extra nice for the money; exceptionally well finished in every detail; a splendid winter garment; retail price would be $1.50; you save at least 40 cents on every one of these garments. Sizes 34 to 46.
Each...$1.10
Per half doz..$6.00
TE 373 Men's Fine Wool Drawers, to match TE 372; same quality and color. These drawers are $1.10 fleeced same as shirts. Sizes, 30 to 46. Each
Per half doz..$6.00

Men's Fleeced Lined Underwear

A Very Strong Line with Us this Year

These are the genuine fleeced lined goods and very much improved in every way over any fleeced goods ever before offered. Fleeced underwear is warmer and stronger than any other style of equal weight. We have some wonderful values quoted.

Special, 50c.

TE 422 Our new medium priced Men's Fleeced Lined Undershirts, heavy winter weight, special fleecing, double stitched flat seams, elastic double cuff; retail price would be 75c; very strong, very warm; color, light brown. 50c
Sizes, 34 to 50. Each ....
Per half doz..$2.85
TE 424 Men's Fleeced Lined Drawers to match TE 422, same style, quality and color. Sizes 30 to 48. 50c
Each...
Per half doz..$2.85

Jersey Ribbed Special, 50c

TE 014 Jersey Ribbed Vests; extra quality cotton yarn, cream color only, special quality Egyptian cotton, extra heavy, silk trimmed; this garment has a light fleecing inside; special value. Sizes, 4, 5 and 6.
Each 50c
Per half doz..$2.85
TE 016 Ladies' Jersey Ribbed Drawers, to match 50c
vests, side buttoned, adjustable band. Each ....
Per half doz..$2.85

Our New Garment Special, 75c

TE 034 M. W. & Co.'s Special Jersey Ribbed Ladies' Vests, ¾ wool, medium heavy weight, fine quality, silk trimmed, natural gray color, superior value. Regular price, $1.00 or more; our price is special on this garment this 75c
season; sizes, 4, 5 and 6. Each....................
TE 036 Ladies' Special Drawers to match TE 034; superior quality at the price. 75c
Sizes 4, 5 and 6. Each..............................
Per half doz..$4.25

These garments are unusual value. Do not overlook them.

Ladies' Union Suit
Special, $1.00

TE 155 Ladies' Union Suits; our best ecru or cream color, made from a special grade of combed Egyptian cotton; heavy winter weight; silk trimmed; a very superior garment. You will be surprised at the extreme value of this garment. The retail price of this quality is $1.37. Our special price. $1.00
Each...

TE 160 Our own make Union Suits; this style is a special value; the material and workmanship are superior, and they are all steam shrunk; made of ¾ wool worsted, ¼ fine cotton, heavy weight, natural gray color, silk trimmed. We offer you this season a much better garment than ever before and at a $1.55
lower price. Per suit ....

Men's Winter Overshirts

Special $1.50

We have an exceptionally strong line of Overshirts, all made to order for us, and guaranteed to be full sizes and well made in all particulars. Remember, we do not sell the ordinary shirts made for the trade, but strictly high-grade goods, made to our order. **Positively better quality at the price than any other firm can possibly offer.**

TE 392—Our Celebrated Blue Denim or Chambray Work Shirt, the perfection of quality and workmanship. Color dark steel blue. This shirt has double front and double back, made of Government standard denim, has yoke shoulder, wide collar, faced sleeves, deep cuff, pearl buttons, gussets, all seams are flat felled and double stitched, bodies are cut extra wide and full length, back and front lining in same material as outside of shirt. Sizes 14½ to 19 inch neck measure. Per ½ dozen...............**$2.87** Each, 50 cents

TE 391—Special quality Men's Overshirt, made of a fine grade heavy weight wool shirting flannel, a splendid winter overshirt, very neat pattern, in light gray, steel blue, light tan stripes or checks, extra well finished, has negligee collar, pocket, pearl buttons, yoke shoulder and gussets. All seams are double stitched. This is one of our standard overshirts for winter wear. Sizes 14½ to 17½ neck measure. Price, each..............**$1.50.** Per ½ doz..............**$8.50**

TE 385—Our New One Dollar Overshirt, made from special winter weight shirting, warm and strong, extra well made, deep collar, 2 pockets, faced sleeves, pearl buttons, yoke shoulders, finished seams, also one string tie of same material with each shirt. Colors, pearl gray, steel blue, or light tan with white stripes and figures. Sizes, 14½ to 17½. Price, each..............**$1.00** Per ½ doz..............**$5.75**

$1.00 TE 385

$1.50 TE 460

TE 362

50c

Special

TE 450—Men's Heavy Weight Blue Flannel Overshirts, strictly first-class in every way—best of workmanship and a good heavy weight, all wool twill sterling flannel; yoke shoulder, double sewed flat felled seams, faced sleeves, negligee collar, pearl buttons, and pocket. This shirt is worth at least $3.00 at retail, and our price is extremely low. Color, navy blue only. Sizes 14½ to 17½ neck measure. Price, each...**$1.50** Per ½ doz..........**$8.75**

Everyone Warranted to Please

You Will Like the Quality in Our Hosiery

Men's Fine Cashmere Half Hose—Winter Weight

25c

These goods are all made from fine all wool yarn, and are not intended for very rough wear or heavy boots; very warm, but also very fine and soft. Average weight, 32 oz. to a dozen. Sizes, 9½ to 11½.

Our Leaders, 25c

TE 380. Men's special value heavy all wool Cashmere Half Hose, English ribbed tops, double heel and toe, full seamless. Color, fast black only; our special stocking; usually sold for 35 to 50 cents. We offer you an exceptional bargain in this stocking; best ever offered at this price.
Per pair......................................25c
Per doz..$2.85

TE 381. Same as TE 380, but color, natural gray. An exceptionally fine stocking this season; very soft and warm, but will wear well. Per pair. **25c**
Per doz.......................................$2.85

Men's Ribbed Leg Shaker Socks. All Wool

TE 412. Men's extra quality good heavy weight Shaker Socks; ribbed legs, our best Shaker, and it is worth much much more than we ask for it. This sock is very soft and warm, and will not irritate the feet like most heavy wool socks. Colors, natural gray or blue. Sizes, 9½ to 11½. Per pair. **42c**
Per doz.......................................$4.75

TE 411. Men's Heavy Shaker Socks, ribbed legs, special value. Regular price, 40 cents. Colors, gray or blue mixed. Sizes 10 to 11½.
Per pair.......................................**29c**
Per doz..$3.25

29c

Our Standard Heavy Weight All Wool Sock

28c

TE 418. Men's Heavy All Wool Sock, our standard quality, almost four pounds to the dozen, close knitted, strong and warm, seamless, and the best value ever offered, really 40-cent retail value. Our price is very special. Colors, blue, natural gray, sheep's gray or scarlet. Sizes 10½ to 12.
Per pair......................................**28c**
Per doz..$3.25

Special

TE 420. Men's Extra Heavy Strictly All Wool Socks, made only for Montgomery Ward & Co., hand finished, seamless, made from scoured wool, hard twisted, close knitted, very strong. They weigh over four pounds to the dozen, and will outlast any other make of winter hosiery. Colors, blue, sheep's gray, natural gray. Sizes, 10½ to 12.
Per pair....................**33c**
Per doz.......................................$3.85

Our Standards of Value

Fleeced Lined Cotton Hose

TE 122. Ladies' Heavy Fleeced Lined Cotton Hose, full regular made, double heel and toe and double sole, a good strong stocking, black, extra quality at this price. Per pair.
25c
Per doz.......................................$2.85

Ladies' Ribbed Leg Hosiery, All Wool, Winter Weight

TE 139. Ladies' Special Quality All Wool Hose, worsted finish, heavy weight, double heel and toe, seamless. This is a strictly first-class stocking. Would be cheap at 50 cents, black only. Per pair.
35c
Per doz.......................................$3.90

$3.00

FE 763

ENTIRE WIDTH 54 INCHES

ENTIRE LENGTH, 66 INCHES

Storm Proof
Wind Proof
Dust Proof
Water Proof

Serviceable Robe & Blanket

Values This is the time to buy them—they will soon be needed. Don't pay two prices! Let us supply you.

PLUSH LAP ROBES

We have the largest number of styles, the greatest variety of patterns, give the best values and sell more robes than any other single house handling this ever-popular class of goods. Plush robes wear well, are warm, and always stylish. All the latest productions of the largest and best plush manufacturers.

"PUSHER" PLUSH ROBE

FE 724 — Our Special Fancy Double Plush Robe. The best robe in the world this season for the price. Two ply of plush; old gold color face, with large tiger medallion center and plain black plush back; handsome all around border; hemmed all around the edge. These robes, if bought through the wholesale jobber and then retailed, could not be offered for less than $4.00 each. Notice our low price. There is an excellent grade of plush in these robes. Size, 48x60 in. Weight, each, 5½ lb. Price, each............**$2.50**

You Can Laugh at the Storm with one of these

Waterproof Lap Robes

Extra Quality, Extra Large.

FE 763—Waterproof Lap Robes, extra large size. Extra quality heavy rubber cloth on the one side, extra quality plain green raised plush on the other side; two rows of stitching all around the edge. These robes are absolutely dust, wind and waterproof, and are positively the best robes of this style that have ever been sold. Size, 54x66 in.; weight, each, 6½ lb. Each..................................**$3.00**

Why buy a cheaper Robe when absolute protection and satisfaction costs only $3.00.

Fur Lap Robes

Here are a few extraordinary bargains

All our Gray Fur Robes are made especially for us from the best selection of imported Japanese goatskins, the seams are all strongly sewed, the skins are well covered with good long hair and every effort is put forth to have each robe thoroughly cleaned and as free from odor as possible.

FE 800—Gray Fur Lap Robes; Japanese goat robe, lined with fancy felt cloth, scalloped border. Size, about 48x60 in. These robes are much superior to the cheap China skins sometimes used in robes of this style. Weight, about 6 lb. Each..................**$3.80**

FE 806—Gray Fur Lap Robes; standard size; Japanese goat fur robes; lined with heavy plush cloth, plain colors, scalloped borders in fancy colors. Size, about 48x60 in. Weight, about 8 lb. Each..............**$5.60**

FE 812 — Gray Fur Robes large size; Japanese goat fur robes, deodorized, lined with extra quality plain plush and trimmed with scalloped felt border. Size, about 51x66 in. Wt., about 10 lbs.

FE 800 Each...**$7.25**

FE 828—Gray Fur Lap Robes, extra large size; Japanese goat fur lap robes, deodorized, lined with the best quality of fancy plush robe lining in figures or medallion patterns, double scalloped borders, extra weight and extra quality. Size, about 60x70 in. Weight, about 13 lb. Each..................**$10.00**

Protect Your Horses

From Severe Weather

Blankets are much Cheaper than Horses

Storm Blankets

Our Storm Blankets are all made especially for us according to our own specifications and are the very best .the market affords in the various styles and sizes. We have had long experience in handling this class of goods and flatter ourselves that we know what is wanted and how to make them, and that we can supply better goods for lower prices than you can possibly obtain elsewhere.

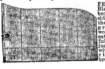

FE 975 Storm Blankets, heavy brown duck outside, lined ⅗ of the width with gray mixed woolen lining, extending the full length; adjustable strap with snap and ring on the breast; gore inserted for the neck on the front end. Size, 76x80 inch; weight, about 4½ lbs. Each.................. **$1.25**

FE 982 Storm Blankets, made of extra heavy brown duck, full lined throughout with heavy fancy mixed gray wool blanket lining; turned back and hemmed all around the edges; rawhide hame leathers, trace straps, 20 rows of stitching, 2 adjustable straps with snaps on the front end. These are absolutely the best storm blankets ever sold for the price. We have sold a great many thousands of them and every one has given the most perfect satisfaction. Size, 76x80 in. Weight, each, 7½ lb. Price, ea. **$2.20**

Square Horse Blankets

Our Horse Blankets have all been very carefully selected, the styles are extremely desirable, the values are the very best the market affords, our prices being lower than regular wholesale jobbing prices on similar qualities. We solicit your orders for Horse Blankets, as we are confident that our goods will please you. Please note that Horse Blankets are not priced by the pair. Each price quoted is for a single blanket.

"Paragon" Square Blankets

Positively and without a doubt the best $1.00 Horse Blanket ever placed on the market.

FE 904 "Paragon" Square Horse Blankets. These blankets are red brown in color with eleven-inch borders in fancy colors and narrow bright colored body stripes, with strap and buckle sewed on front end. The stock is clean, the colors are bright and attractive and our price by the single blanket is lower than wholesale dealers ask for a similar quality; Size, 76x80 in. Weight, each, 5 lbs. Price, each..... **$1.00**

"Empress" Square Horse Blankets

Extra Quality, Size and Weight.

FE 912 "Empress" Square Horse Blankets. Very clean, bright goods and splendid value. These blankets are made upon honor throughout with good clean stock, very strong hard twisted warps and are warranted for service and durability. Red brown body with four rows of three-color stripes and solid fancy headings in five colors. These blankets are very showy and are guaranteed to give perfect satisfaction. Sewed strap. Size, 84x90 in. Weight, each, 6 lbs. Price, each.................. **$1.50**

Our Dandy Single Harness $11.00

Lowest price ever made on a Harness of this quality

Per Set . . . . . .

$11.00 for a high-grade set of harness that cannot be purchased anywhere else for less than $15.00, and some merchants would not hesitate about asking $18.00 or $20.00.

The **Dandy Harness at $11.00** represents a rare bargain. It is not a commonplace set picked up in the open market and offered by us at agood profit price. It took our harness buyer, a man of over 15 years' experience, many weeks to perfect an arrangement with a manufacturer whereby we can offer this high-grade, nobby harness at the low price of $11.00.

It's all in the quality. We could, if we desired, sell a set that looks like the Dandy at many dollars less, but that is not what we are trying to do. Anybody can make alow price on a second-rate article, but it takes clever buying and expert knowledge to be able tosell areally topnotch article at a price lower than many firms can buy the same article for. In the Dandy Harness at $11.00weofferwhat we knew to be the best set of single driving harness ever put on the market for less than $15.00.

Is not this a Beauty?

Now that the year's work is almost done you will have plenty of opportunities to use a good buggy harness. Why not order one of these? Just to acquaint yourself with Ward values.

You never saw the equal of this Harness elsewhere for less than

$15.00

FE 88—Montgomery Ward & Co.'s Special Single Buggy Harness. This harness is made from selected oak tanned leather, trimmed with the very best qualities of mountings in the different finishes; is made by the most skillful workmen in the country, and every set is absolutely guaranteed to give perfect satisfaction to every purchaser. We cannot speak too highly of the many good qualities of this style, which is made for average size horses weighing from 900 lbs. to 1200 lbs. each. At our low price of $11.00 per set this harness is a world beater, as the regular retail value is at least $15.00 per set.

The following is a brief description of our Dandy harness, which is heavy, strong and substantial:

BRIDLE—⅝ in., box loops, patent leather blinds, round winker stay, layer on crown, overcheck with nose-band or open bridle if preferred. BREAST COLLAR—Extra wide, V-shaped, TRACES—1¼ in., stitched to breast collar, scalloped and raised points. BREECHING—1⅛ in., side straps, ⅜ in., hip strap, ⅝ in., turnback, ⅞ in., scalloped, round crupper sewed on. SADDLE—3 in., single strap, harness leather skirts, patent leather jockeys, swell shaped pad with leather bottom, doubled and stitched bearers. BELLYBAND—Griffith style, long billets for shafts. LINES—1 in., to loop in; all black leather. HITCH REIN—⅝ in., with snap. Made for average horses weighing from 900 to 1200 lbs. each.

Best quality of nickel on composition mountings or imitation rubber mountings if preferred.
Per set..................................$11.00

With genuine rubber mountings.
Per set.................................. 13.00

For harness of this quality, suitable for heavier horses weighing from 1200 to 1600 lbs., add per set......$1.25
Weight, per set, packed in box, about 24 lb.

Remarkable Harness Values

No other firm ever equaled our prices on these qualities and the average Harness dealer would ask about one-half more.

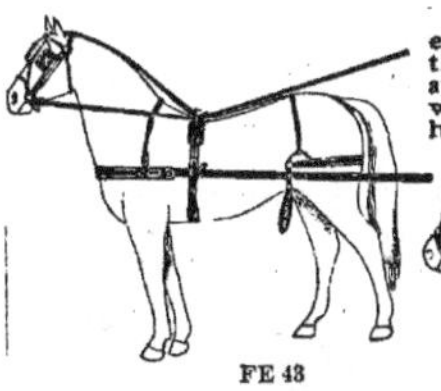

FE 43

FE 101

FE 396

Our $10.00 Single Harness

FE 43—Single Buggy Harness; imitation hand sewed. The best harness in the world for the price. We recommend this harness to any one desiring a neat appearing, well made and serviceable single harness at a moderate price. One hitch strap with each harness. Open bridles furnished when ordered. SADDLE, 3 in. single strap harness, leather skirts, leather lined pad; BRIDLE, ⅝-in., box loops, patent leather winkers, round winker braces, overdraw with nose band or round side checks; TRACES, 1½-in., 6 ft. long, doubled, raised and stitched, to buckle to breast collar; LINES, ⅞-in. with 1-in. hand parts; BREAST COLLAR, folded with straight raised layer and box loops for traces and neck straps; BREECHING, folded with straight raised layer; BELLYBANDS, folded, Griffith style; side straps, ⅞ in.; turnback waved with round crupper; hip straps, ⅝ in.; no martingales; full nickel mounting or imitation rubber mounting if preferred. Suitable for average horses weighing up to 1,200 lbs. Per set..**$10.00**

Hames and collar in place of breast collar, extra....................................... 1.50

Round lines in place of flat lines, extra...... 1.00

For harness large enough for horses weighing from 1,200 to 1,600 lbs. add $1.25.

FE 43 harness with breast collar weighs 24 lbs., packed in box for shipping.

Our Fine Brass Trimmed Single Buggy Harness

Suitable for horses from 900 to 1,200 lbs.

FE 101—Our Fine Brass Trimmed Single Buggy Harness. Made from No. 1 selected oak-tanned leather, finely and smoothly finished, heavy, solid, strong and substantial and trimmed with solid brass mountings. BRIDLE, ⅝ in., overcheck, box loop, round winker stays, layer on crown, nose band; BREAST COLLAR, extra wide, "V"-shaped center, heavy stock; TRACES, 1¼ in., heavy stock, stitched to breast collar; BREECHING, 1⅜ in., side straps ⅞ in., hip strap ⅝ in., turn-back ⅞ in., scalloped, round crupper; SADDLE, 3 in., single strap skirts, swell, patent leather jockeys, 10 in. fancy bound housings, leather bottom pads, metal bearer loops; BELLYBAND, "Griffith" style, long shaft billets; LINES, ⅞ in. fronts with spring billets, 1⅛ in. hand parts. One hitch strap. First-class stock with smooth round edge finish all through. Every set of this harness is warranted to give satisfaction. Full brass mountings. Per set.....**$12.00**

Weight, per set, packed in box, about 25 lbs.

Double Ruggy Harness

FE 396—Double buggy harness, imitation hand sewed. Good stock, well made, smoothly finished and splendid value. BRIDLES, ⅝ in., box loops on checks, three rows stitched, patent leather winkers, round winker braces, layer on crown, overcheck, chain fronts, rosettes and bits; HAMES, 7 lb., iron with japanned body and plated terrets; Martingale, ⅞ in.; hame tugs, 1⅛ in., patent leather, swell ends, with box loops; TRACES, 1⅛ in., 6 ft. 4 in. long, doubled and stitched, with round edge finish; POLE STRAPS, 1¼ in., full length, heavy stock; CHOKE STRAPS, ⅞ in.; PADS, leather bound, 1⅛ in., single strap skirts, doubled and stitched bearers and billets; BELLYBANDS, folded; turnbacks ¾-in. single strap, scalloped, with stuffed round cruppers sewed on; LINES, ⅞ in. throughout; COLLARS, gig weight, all black. Mention sizes wanted. Two hitch reins. Full nickel mountings or imitation rubber mountings if preferred. Per set.......**$20.00**

Weight, per set, in box, about 37 lbs.

Breast collars in place of hames and collars same price. For single hip-strap breeching, add..:.....$4.65

Halters

We carry a large and complete line of halters and give better value than any other house in the country.

FE 800—Black Leather Halters, 5-ring, copper riveted, 1-in. head, without tie strap. Wt., 20 oz. Each........**60c.**

FE 802—Black Leather Halters, copper riveted, 5-ring, 1-in. head, with tie strap. Wt., 24 oz. Each......**94c.**

FE 804—Black Leather Halters, 5-ring, copper riveted, 1¼-in. head, without tie strap, Wt., 24 oz. Each.......**70c.**

FE 806—Black Leather Halters, copper riveted, 5-ring, 1¼ in. head, with heavy tie strap, Each...................**$1.10**

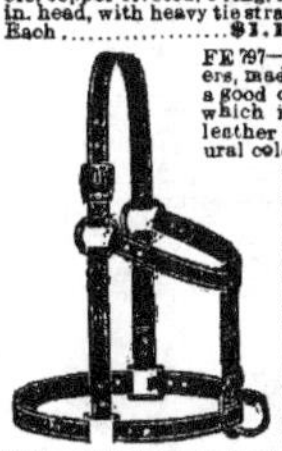

FE 797—Russet Leather Horse Halters, made in the "6-Ring" style from a good quality of tanned rawhide, which is finished with a regular leather tannage and left in the natural color, large size, all parts 1 in. wide and all securely made with heavy coppered finish tubular rivets. We are unable to supply tie straps to match. Weight, each, 16 oz. Price, each............**49c.** Per doz.................$4.65

FE 798—Extra quality Russet Leather Horse Halters, made in the "6-Ring" style from a special selection of heavy rawhide, which is finished with a regular leather tannage and left in the natural leather color. All parts are 1¼-in. wide and are securely fastened by heavy coppered tubular rivets. These halters are large size and are heavy, strong and substantial. They can only be supplied in one style and without tie straps. Weight, each, 23 oz. Price, per doz..$7.25. Each **62c**

Enjoy the Winter

You need a little fun after
the summer's hard work

Strongest and Best $11.90
For the Money "Samson" Four-Knee Bob-sled. $11.90 at Chicago.

JE 1105—Our "Samson" Bobsled is offered to our customers with the assurance that a better bob of its kind cannot be obtained at any price. We sell it under our guarantee for one year against defective material or workmanship. It is made under our own supervision, none but the best clear straight-grain, well seasoned timber being used, the bracing being very heavy and carefully put on, so as to properly divide the strain. The painting is a special mixture upon which a great deal of time has been spent, with a view to making it weather-proof. We use the best quality of varnish, and the sled will retain its nice appearance for several seasons. The runners are 2 in. wide by 3 in. deep, made of rock elm, the toughest and best material for the purpose. Knees, 2¼x2¾ in. Reaches, 1½x2¾ in. Bolsters, 3½x4¼ in. Tongue, 3½x3½ in. Raves, 1½x5½ in. The bracing is a good quality of Bessemer steel, the tongue bracing being ½x1½ in., the reach braces ⅜x1¼ in., knee braces, 3-16x1¼ in., and the knee irons on end of runners 1½ in., No. 14 steel. Bolsters are regularly furnished for bed 38 in. wide. Track, 3 ft. 2 in. Painting, nice shade of red, nicely striped. Shipping weight 380 lbs. Order No. JE 1105. Price at Chicago...... **$11.90**
Extra for bolsters for 42 in. wagon box..............60c
"Samson" 6 Knee. Price at Chicago............**$13.50**

The above sleds are good in every way, in fact we do not know where to buy better. We can get for you, if you desire it, a sled with smaller size runners, knees, reaches, bolsters and tongue for $1.00 less than the prices given above. Should you order this kind, order **Samson Jr.**

At the Price We Offer Our
"Surprise" Portland Cutter $16.95
You Can Afford One

95c
off
on all orders for the "Surprise" Portland received & shipped before Nov. 15, 1904.

Air seasoned timber.
Good workmanship.
Removable trimmings.

Nicely
Finished

JE 1006—A good, strong, roomy Portland Cutter, made of carefully selected material throughout, strongly braced gear, with durable trimmings and fine finish; all new stock, nicely proportioned body, and at a price $8.00 to $10.00 less than the same cutter could be purchased for locally. WOODWORK—Ash frame, veneered panels, 3-ply dash, rock elm runners; bent hickory knees, hickory beams. IRONWORK—Steel braces, clipped to knees; wrought iron bolts and clips; channel steel shoes turned up at heel; strong step plates. TRIMMING—Regularly trimmed in a good quality wool green cloth (whipcord at the same price when so ordered). Seat cushion, back and sides are removable for storage during summer months. PAINTING—Body nicely finished, the upper part of side panels in bronze green to match gear, and the lower part in rich black. Running gear and inside of dash in bronze green with neat striping. SIZES—Seat, 35 inches on bottom; cushion, 36 inches on top. Back, 22 inches high from seat bottom. Panels, 9½ inches high at front post. Gear, 17 inches high. Track, 3 feet 2 inches from out to out. EQUIPMENT—Nickel-plated arm rails and line rail; carpet on bottom; whip socket; foot scrapers; selected hickory shafts with shifting bar. Weight, about 190 lbs. Customer pays freight from factory in southern Michigan. Order No. JE 1006. Price with shafts and shifting bar.......... **$16.95**
Extra for pole in place of shafts $1.75; Extra for velvet plush trimming, $1.50

Our Most Popular

Dining Chairs

Beautifully Hand-Carved

Prices 'Way Down

RE 58½. A new and very showy Wood Seat Dining-Room Chair. Made very comfortable and strong. The most comfortable wood seat set in America. Large seats and extra well made. Has strong brace arm. Nicely finished in golden. Weight about 12 lb. Per doz. $13.25
Each **$1.15**

RE 59 Men's Armchair to match RE 58½. Made strong, with large high arms. No dining-room set should be without an armchair for head of the house.
Each, only **$2.50**
A set of five diners and armchair for **$7.75**

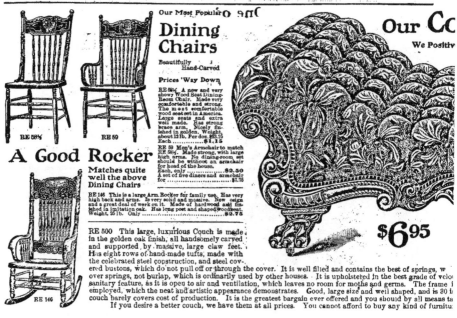

RE 58½   RE 59

A Good Rocker

Matches quite well the above Dining Chairs

RE 146 This is a large Arm Rocker for family use. Has very high back and arms. Is very solid and massive. New design and a great deal of work on it. Made of hardwood and finished in imitation oak. Has long post and shaped wood seat. Weight, 26 lb. Only **$2.75**

RE 146

Our Co

We Positiv

$6.95

RE 500 This large, luxurious Couch is made in the golden oak finish, all handsomely carved and supported by massive, large claw feet. Has eight rows of hand-made tufts, made with the celebrated steel construction, and steel covered buttons, which do not pull off or through the cover. It is well filled and contains the best of springs, w over springs, not burlap, which is ordinarily used by other houses. It is upholstered in the best grade of velo sanitary feature, as it is open to air and ventilation, which leaves no room for moths and germs. The frame i employed, which the neat and artistic appearance demonstrates. Good, large size and well shaped, and is 30 i couch barely covers cost of production. It is the greatest bargain ever offered and you should by all means ta
If you desire a better couch, we have them at all prices. You cannot afford to buy any kind of furnitu

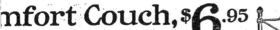

Combination Divan, Sofa, or Couch
One of the Handiest Pieces of Furniture ever invented

This illustration shows head and foot raised, making a fine sofa or davenport

Our Price for this Handy Couch is only

12⁵⁰

Made of Solid Oak

RE 195
This illustration shows head and foot lowered, making a luxurious couch.

This handsome and useful piece is made of solid oak — golden or weathered finish. Also in mahogany finish, if desired. It is constructed in such a manner that the arms can be adjusted to seven different positions. Either arm can be lowered or raised to any angle to serve as head of couch. In this way it enables you to use the right or left arm as the head of couch, which is a great advantage over the ordinary couch, and no complicated mechanism to get out of order. It is exceedingly strong and substantially made and shipped with back off, which is a great saving in freight. It is easily handled and quickly set up. Has large, heavy carved feet, castored and upholstered in five-tone velour plush in the latest patterns.

Can be furnished in green (as illustrated), or in dark red. Made with spring edges and guaranteed construction, with a heavy canvas duck bottom. It is in every way a most desirable and useful piece of furniture. When used as a sofa, with arms up, it is 55 inches long. When arms are extended, and it is used as a couch, it is 78 in. long.

Depth of seat, 25 inches. Weight, packed for shipment, 97 lb. It would cost you at least double our price in many stores. Order No. RE 195. Our **$12.50** price. complete, packed for shipment, ▼ only..........................

Davenport Sofa Bed

A more useful or handy piece of high-grade Furniture was never made.

15⁹⁵

Combination Davenport Sofa Beds. The popularity of this piece has continued throughout many years. With all the beauty of a sofa by day they combine the advantages of a restful, comfortable bed by night. Added to this is the additional feature of gates which swing out and form complete head and foot boards exactly the same as a bed. When opened as a bed they are like luxurious couches. As a Davenport they afford a splendid opportunity for artistic decoration, and enrich and dignify an interior more than any one article of household use.

RE 205. Closed—As a Davenport Sofa.

RE 205 Waldorf Sofa Bed. No more useful, at the same time ornamental, piece of furniture has ever been made than the Waldorf Sofa Bed. Only a few seconds are necessary to change it from a beautiful sofa to a full sized, comfortable sofa bed. The framework of this style is exceptionally tasty. When closed the sofa is 77 in. long and 33 in. wide. When back is down it is 48 in. wide, in that way making practically a full sized bed. The cut showing the bed open shows that the ends which are hinged on the side produce a full sized head and foot piece. The framework is either of oak finished in golden, weathered or Antwerp, or selected birch finished and polished in mahogany. Weight, 150 lb. Grade F, corduroy or figured velour velvet plush

RE 205. Open — As a Bed.

15⁹⁵

An Old Time Favorite

400 of these Desks sold in 1901, 2,000 in 1902, 4,500 in 1903. This year we ordered and will sell

6,000 Writing Desks at 3⁹⁵

Description—A Large, Roomy, Family Writing Desk and Bookcase Combined, 5 feet high and 30 inches wide, has a drop leaf made of polished oak, size 18¾x28¾ in., and inside is nicely arranged with pigeon holes sufficient for a large family correspondence and account keeping. Below the drop leaf are two large spaces for books and on the top are shelves for bric-a-brac, photos and other family keepsakes. Top is also fitted with an oval bevel mirror, which adds to the attractiveness of the desk. It is made of oak, highly finished, with golden oak finished (lower) shelves. RE 46 Price, desk only, without curtain.....

3⁹⁵

Shipped direct from factory in North'n Wisconsin. Only a few of the 6,000 left. This offer good only while present stock lasts.

Cut Your Fodder

and sell your hay.

"Chicago" Feed Cutter

Bolted Frame. The Best Cutter of this Size Made.

$6<u>**25**</u> **At Chicago, or Warehouse at Toledo, Ohio.**

EE 954—This is the strongest, most complete, and in fact the best cheap feed cutter made. It is very simple and extremely durable, the cutting-knife is 11½ inches long, made of tempered tool steel, and makes a downward, shearing cut against a hardened cutting edge. It is quickly adjustable to cut ⅜ in., 1 in., 1½ in., or 2 inches, and makes 3 cuts to one turn of the crank. Shaft is ⅞ inch cold rolled steel. Balance wheel is large and heavy, making it easy to run. Feeding device: It has a fluted roll which turns and moves up the fodder the proper distance, and will stop until the knife passes again. Capacity about 150 to 200 pounds of dry fodder, 300 to 400 pounds green fodder per hour. Weight 165 lbs. Price, **$6.25**

Extra knives, each..65

Treats for the boys

Have You one of the Circulars

IF NOT, WRITE FOR A COPY

Address: "TREAT" MANAGER

MONTGOMERY WARD & CO.

CHICAGO

"Dandy" Corn Sheller.

5000 sold in 1904.

EE 750—We sell thousands of these little shellers every season, and the demand is growing. There are a dozen or more kinds, somewhat similar in appearance, but there is considerable difference in the construction, material, and the work they do. Our sheller is the original "Dandy," and is easily the best sheller of this style on the market. Is adjustable to large or small ears of corn, and does first-class work. It is made of the best material, very carefully fitted. Has spring tension, large perfect picker wheel, is made heavy and strong, and gives perfect satisfaction. Every one guaranteed. The price is exceedingly low, considering the quality of this sheller. Weight, 15 lbs. Price...................................**70c**

The Man Who Farms

with his brains as well as his hands seldom complains. Grind your feed. Fatten your stock quickly at minimum cost.

$10<u>**20**</u> **At Chicago, or Factory —in Central Ohio—**

"Lightning" Grinding Mill

One of the best selling mills we have, especially adapted for power windmills and other light power. It has always given our trade splendid satisfaction.

EE 994—Is made of iron and steel, has few wearing parts, is not liable to get out of order, will not choke up, will run empty without injury to burrs. The burrs are so arranged that if nails or any other hard substance gets into the grain they will pass through without breaking the mill. Grinds all kinds of shelled and small grains. Will grind from 6 to 16 bushels per hour if run from 600 to 1,200 revolutions per minute. Requires 2 to 4 horse-power. Can be run by geared windmills or any other power. The burrs are 6¼ inches in diameter and accurately fitted. Pulley, 6¼ in. in diameter; 4-in. face. Such a mill usually sells for $12 to $15. Weight, 90 pounds. **$10.20** Mill with coarse burrs in, and with extra set of fine burrs.............
Extra burrs, per pair (state whether fine or coarse).......................75

A Reliable $8.00 Sheller for $4.95

"Ohio" Original Round-Nose Sheller
Bolted Frame

Look over the description and then look over the Sheller that sells locally for $7 and $8. You can not find 5c difference in the quality.

EE 767 Price, with fan and feed table, at Chicago...**$4.95**

Price extra for 8 in. diameter pulley so that the sheller can be run by light power .... .75

When it is run by power the speed should be about the same as when run by hand; if not shelled corn will be thrown out with the cob.

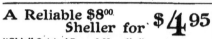

$4.95

at Chicago

This Sheller combines every desirable feature to make it a perfect machine of its kind. It is strong, easy running, an excellent separator and cleaner. The FRAME WORK is made of heavy hardwood and is strongly bolted together, making the machine firm and rigid. A Sheller put together as this one costs a little more money than if nailed or screwed together, and will last twice as long as the latter. PANELS are heavy material. SHAFTS are heavy, cold-rolled steel and run in iron bearings run through and bolted to the frame. BALANCE WHEEL is very large. FAN is metal. FEED SPOUT is placed directly over shelling wheel, which grips the ears of corn firmly. The RAG IRON and the SPRINGS are adjustable and can be set close to the shelling wheel for small corn and leave the spring flexible for large corn to pass through without using so much power. SHELLING-WHEELS are geared high so as to give it good capacity. We guarantee the sheller not to choke. Furnished with fan, which takes all the dirt and puts the corn in marketable condition. Capacity, from 10 to 15 bushels per hour. Weight, about 135 lbs.

Will Pay for Itself
in a season

Every home should have one

"Family" Grist Mill
Have Fresh Graham Flour, Cornmeal, Hominy, Etc.

$1.95

EE 964 If you own one of these mills you can have at all times fresh Graham flour, cornmeal, hominy, split peas, cracked wheat, fine table or butter salt; in fact, everything that is ground at a custom mill except fine bolted family flour. Can be adjusted to grind fine or coarse. Has heavy balance wheel, making it run easy. It is not necessary to throw THIS mill away because the burrs are worn out, for they can be replaced at any time for only 95 cents. The grinding surfaces are of a very hard material, ground off perfectly true; burrs 4½ in. in diameter. Can be attached to box or table. Weight, 30 lbs. Each.... **$1.95**

Extra burrs, per pair, weight, 1 lb. .55

The Hen that Lays is the Hen that Pays

You should have our "Ohio" Bone Cutter if you have chickens

$4.95

"Ohio" No. 4 Green Bone Cutter

EE 820 THOROUGHLY WELL MADE AND GUARANTEED TO DO PERFECT WORK. Strong where strength is required, all superfluous weight being avoided by using best possible materials throughout. A green bone 4x6½ may be thrown into the hopper and cut up without clogging. Case-hardened drop-forged cutter-head, possessing the best possible wearing and cutting qualities; will cut effectually the hardest bone, the toughest gristle, making all very fine and adapted for food. These mills cut the bone like meal, leaving no chunks to lodge in the crop. Automatic feed, and may also be used to cut vegetables. Can cut with right or left hand. The No. 4 Cutter is a genuine record breaker for ease of operation, quality of work and speed, readily cutting out a hopper full by hand (2¼ lbs.) in two or three minutes, enough for a flock of 60 or 70 hens for one day, and fine enough for little chicks. At Chicago. Weight, 26 lbs., with crank, without stand.... **$4.95**

With balance wheel instead of crank, weight, 46 lbs. 6.90
Price extra cutter heads.... .90

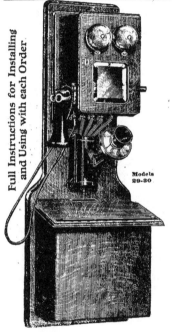

Models
29-30

We positively state, without hesitation or fear of successful contradiction, that our Telephones are reliable, will give you entire satisfaction, and are the lowest priced Instruments on the market, quality considered.

$12.25 Bridging Instrument

For use on private or party lines.

A high grade, perfect working Bridging Telephone for $12.25 with 1,000-ohm ringer movement. We fully guarantee the Diamond Telephones. They satisfy everywhere. If there is a line already in operation in your neighborhood, and you wish to go in on it, no matter if the instruments in use are not of our make, you can use the Diamond Bridging phones on the line. Diamond phones work equally well in connection with instruments of other makes.

KE 2 Specifications: Five-bar steel magnet bridging generator, full nickel plate; long pattern ringer bridging movement, full nickel plate; plate glass front to magneto door; long lever automatic switch; platinum contacts; long distance solid back transmitter; adjustable transmitter arm, with concealed cords; long distance induction coil; bi-polar receiver and cord; two cells, dry or liquid battery; handsomely finished cabinet, finished in oak or walnut, with wide battery box; bi-polar lightning arrester, diamond type. Price, with 1,000 ohm ringer movement, each..........$12.25
Price, with 1,600-ohm ringer movement, each...................................... 12.75
Price, with 1,800-ohm ringer movement, each...................................... 13.35

Diamond Bridging Telephone. Model 30.

KE 10 - Exactly the same as KE 2, except that is furnished with our Jumbo 6-Bar Generator.
Price, with 1,000-ohm ringer movement, each.......................................$13.75
Price, with 1,600-ohm ringer movement, each...................................... 14.25
Price, with 2,000-ohm ringer movement, each...................................... 14.75

Stockman's Quick Draw Tourist's Glass $10⁰⁰

Our own special importation

A superior glass in every way and splendid value for the money. Note the special features. Price includes leather case and shoulder strap. 3,000 sold last year.

KE 312—This glass has a patented spring quick draw adjustment. Besides the focusing wheel it is provided with a quick draw sliding tube telescopic adjustment and is operated by sliding out to fullest extent and obtaining correct focus by using focus wheel. This affords a very quick focus. When observation is finished tubes may be closed instantly without altering the focus already obtained. Measures 4¼ in. closed and 6 in. extended. Weight, about 2 lbs. Finely finished in black enamel and black morocco; perfect optical construction. Body provided with extension sun shades, lenses achromatic of highest grade, giving clearest definition and magnifying 6½ times. Complete with leather carrying case and shoulder strap. Price, **$10.00** (postage 40c).

HANDY AND CHEAP HOUSEHOLD SCALE 93c

CE 773—Household Scale is beautifully made of steel throughout and absolutely unbreakable; has large white enamel dial; very distinct and serviceable. Enameled steel top plate. By means of the top adjusting screw it can be instantly adjusted to make proper allowance for a basket or pan. Capacity, 24 lb. by oz. Fully warranted. Weight, boxed, 3¾ lbs. Each............**93c**

CE 774—Household Scale, same as above but fitted with fork instead of top plate, complete with strong tin scoop. Weight, 3⅞ lbs. Each....**$1.00.**
CE 774½—Household Scale, same as CE 773 but fitted with fork instead of top plate, compl't. with polished brass scoop. Weight, 4 lbs. Each....**$1.25**

A SCIENTIFIC ROASTER AND BAKER 47c

We claim it to be the best and most perfect in the market for two reason that it is self basting, as all steam and moisture is retained in pan when closed and all condensation from top of pan drips over the meat. The roast is made in its own steam, will be of greater weight, more juicy and retain better flavor than in any other pan. It stands on heavy runners. It has a good rack to keep the meat from becoming soaked. It is made of fine smooth steel. Try one and you will never regret it.

CE 783—Size.	Length.	Width.	Height.	Weight.	Each.
2	15 in.	10	7	3 lb. 14 oz.	$0.47
3	16 in.	11	8¼	4 lb. 7 oz.	.56
4	18¾ in.	13½	8¼	5 lb. 3 oz.	.67

5,000 Sets to be Sold

At 58 cents for this excellent Door Bell Set, we expect to sell them by the thousands, and will be disappointed if we don't sell at least 5,000 sets from this catalogue. 58 cents complete, as described below. One of the best bargains in Electrical Goods we have ever seen.

Our Special Electric Door Bell Set

Consisting of
One Good Grade Electric Bell   One Wood Push Button   One Package Staples
One Dry Battery   50 Feet Insulated Wire   One Piece Tape
K E 773—Can you beat it at our price?   Per set..................... **58c**

The "Emergency" Electric Vest-Pocket Light . . . **70c**

Polished nickel trimmings, finely finished cover. Can be carried in vest-pocket. This Emergency Light is not a toy. It gives instant light. No heat, matches, trouble or danger. No wires to go wrong. Cannot be blown out by the wind. Useful to clergymen on night calls. Farmers going into dark stables, granaries, root houses, etc. Miners, going into dangerous mines. Plumbers, who have to examine leaking gas pipes in dark places. Railroad employes of all classes. Bookkeepers and bank employes, who have to find books, etc., in dark vaults. Many uses about the house at night. Used in U. S. and British Navies, as well as in many other government services of foreign countries. A child can operate the Emergency Vest-Pocket Flash Light. Gives 2,000 to 3,000 flashes before exhausting battery. Postage extra, 10c.
KE 077 — With pressed board case. Mfr's. price, $1.00. Our price......... **70c**
KE079—With leatherette covered case. Mfr's price, $1.25 .Our price.. 90c
KE081—Our special compressed fibre polished case. Impervious to water. Mfr's. price. $1.50. Our price $1.10
Extra Batteries......................... 25c
Extra Bulbs 35c

A Handsome, Efficient and Popular Family Medical Battery

Voltamp Battery No. 9

KE 352—Although one of the smallest instruments of Voltamp manufacture, the same care and precision is exercised in its construction as with the high-priced apparatus. The current strength will be found amply sufficient for family use. This instrument furnishes three currents—primary, secondary and combined. Put up in a handsomely finished oak case. The convenient form of this instrument makes it especially attractive, combining many features of superiority. Two conducting cords, two nickel-plated handle electrodes, one rosewood handle, one sponge holder, foot-plate and copy of complete electro-medical treatise, "Faradic Hints." Dimensions, 8¾x6¼x 5¼ inches. Weight 5½ lbs.
Price, complete, as shown in cut......... **$3.25**

Extra dry batteries for above..................... 25c

Light for all

We have lamps from 17 cents to $17.00 each. The variety is endless. These are our greatest sellers. Every one a favorite. We have every variety and style, the product of the best makers in the country.

Our lamps are splendid light givers.

BE 407 We have selected this burner (after a careful comparison with all others) as being the very best to be procured for the money. Try one and you will be more than pleased. No. 2 Chief 80-Candle Power Central Draft Stand Lamp complete, with opal dome shade, 10-in. shade holder and chimney; height to top of chimney, 20 in.; takes No. 2 Rochester round wick and chimney. Why use an inferior lamp when one guaranteed by a reputable firm can be purchased at price quoted? Order one, and return at our expense if it does not bear out the following description: 1st, gives strong, steady white light; 2d, easiest wicking device invented; 3d, wick never sticks and can be raised and lowered instantly; 4th, well made and shapely throughout. Weight, packed, 16 lb.................................... **$1.50**

BE 303

BE 407

Our line is complete, with a larger range of styles than carried elsewhere, and at the lowest possible prices, quality considered. We use the B. & H. burner on all our center draft hanging lamps, which is acknowledged best made.

Hanging lamps are not furnished with hooks with which to hang.

BE 301 Polished bronze metal, rich gold finish, Hanging Lamp, improved spring extension; length, closed. 30 in.; extended, 66 in. Complete with 14-in. plain white dome shade, glass oil pots and No. 3 sun burner, 1¾-in. wick and No. 2 sun chimney. Weight, packed, 30 pounds. Price........ **$1.95**

BE 303 Polished Bronze Metal Hanging Lamp, rich gold finish, patent improved extension; length, closed, 30 in.; extended, 66 in. Fancy hand decorated 14-in. dome shade and fount to match on pure white background, complete with chimney and climax burner, 1¾-in. wick and No. 2 sun chimney. Weight, packed, 30 pounds. Each **$2.55**

BE 368 This is a new creation done by the celebrated Kopp, and is destined to be one of the most popular lamps of the season. The globe, which is 10 inches in diameter, and body of lamp are in the form of a huge pineapple in cerise at bottom, shading to pink at center, and surmounted with green leaves at top; trimmed with fancy rich gold open work foot, spun polished brass oil pot fitted with Success 80-candle power burner, which takes No. 1 Belgian chimney and wick. Height, to top of chimney, 22 inches. Weight, packed, about 20 lb. This is a new and very attractive lamp at a low price. Each **$2.45**

BE 301

BE 368

Built for Service

$6.50

Our Trunks will stand the strain

We are the largest handlers of Trunks in the United States and are the only mail order house handling this line, which is the product of the largest trunk factory in the world. You can therefore readily see why our quality is best, prices lowest.

BE 374 Canvas covered, large flat top, slightly bulged, fancy japanned iron binding and center band, heavy leather straps, four hardwood slats running full length of top and two around body, heavy brass-plated corners, clamps, knees and valance clamps, brass excelsior lock, heavy sliding leather handles, steel hinges, heavily protected iron bottom, deep tray with two compartments, cover hinged on back and center cloth faced, extra dress tray.

Size.	Weight.	Each.	Size.	Weight.	Each.	Size.	Weight.	Each.
30 in.	45 lbs.	$6.50	34 in.	55 lbs.	$7.50	38 in.	65 lbs.	$8.60
32 in.	50 lbs.	7.00	36 in.	60 lbs.	8.00	40 in.	75 lbs.	9.25

Florence Chamber Set

Genuine English Stone China, pure white, good and substantial. Not decorated but heavily embossed and may be used with any colored furnishings. The shape is good, sizes large and the price very low for first quality imported iron stone china. Set complete as illustrated, consisting of bowl and pitcher, covered chamber, mug and soap slab. Weight, packed, 30 lbs. Per set $1.52

Think of it! This handsome set for only . . . .

$1.52

46-Piece Glass Set $1 95
Prism Pattern

Prism Pattern Glassware
The Prism Pattern is the brightest, neatest, best finished low-priced pattern produced this season. The quality is good, pure, crystal glass. The illustration is a correct reproduction of the ware. It will give good service at a very low price and will be sure to please any one.

Did you ever see such a bargain before?

While this is a remarkably low priced assortment and worthy your consideration, if you need a full set, we do not compel you to take the full set, as many catalogue houses do; we will be glad to sell you any part at prices quoted:

BE 677—Doz., 25c
BE 671—17c
BE 683—7c
BE 675 Doz., 35c
BE 679—10c
BE 673—Doz., 45c
BE 619—Set, 4 pcs., 25c
BE 685—25c
BE 681—20c
BE 687—6c

BE 687½   Complete set as follows: 1 Table Set, 4 pieces; 1 Water Pitcher, 1 doz. Tumblers, 1 doz. Wine Glasses, 1 high Covered Fruit Bowl, 1 Jelly Stand, 1 Cake Salver, 1 doz. Sauce or Berry Dishes, 1 Nappy, 8 in.; 1 Pickle Dish.   46 pieces.   Weight, 30 lbs.. **$1.95**

Cold Blast Storm Lantern $1 00

BE 634 Cold Blast Storm Dash or Farm Wagon Lantern; will not blow out in the strongest wind; can be used either on front of wagon, or if hung underneath will throw a good light ahead of the team. It is fitted with a No. 2 burner, taking a 1-inch wick. Weight, 3 lbs. Per doz., $10.80.
Each..**$1.00**

Beautiful Water Set 95c

BE 776 New Tankard Shape Water Set. Body is crystal glass with tinted panels enameled in various colored flowers, edges of all pieces are trimmed with gold. A good, medium priced set, consists of one ½-gallon pitcher, six ½-pint tumblers, and 13-inch fancy polished white metal tray. Weight, 5 lbs.
Per set.................................**95c**

Stationery, Leather Goods and Game Bargains

Writing Tablets.

IMMENSE PENCIL TABLET, ONLY 4 CENTS

HE 508 "Clipper" Pencil Tablet, 7x10 in., containing 125 sheets smooth white paper ruled for pencil use. Immense value at the price. Shipping weight, 14 oz. Per doz.......... $0.42

Per gross.................. 4.90

Each.................. **4c**

"MADISON" WRITING TABLETS EQUAL MANY WHICH RETAIL AT 10 CENTS EACH.

"Madison" Writing Tablets numbers HE 542 to HE 547, contain smooth finish, white writing paper, ruled both sides; tinted cover, printed in colors, with blotter attached. GREATEST VALUE IN MARKET AT THE PRICE. Shipping weight each, 10 oz.

	Size.	Sheets.	Per gross.	Per doz.	Each.
HE 542 — Commercial Note......	5 x 8	120	$5.10	$0.45	$0.04
HE 546 — P'ket Note..	5½ x 9	60	5.10	.45	.04
HE 547 — Letter......	8 x 10	65	5.10	.45	.04

HE 738 Woman's Crush Belt, of black faille corded silk, with two rows crocheted button ornaments on back and gilt prong harness buckle; width 3½ in. at back, tapering to 1 in. in front. Sizes, 24 to 30 in. Mention waist measure when ordering. Each.......... **45c**

Woman's "Apollo" Satin Belt.

HE 791 Woman's Tucked Belt, of double faced black satin, with gold-plated back piece and prong buckle; 5 in. wide at back, 2½ in. in front. Sizes, 24 to 30 in. Mention waist measure when ordering. Shipping weight, 5 oz. Each.................. **$1.00**

Great Western $1.00 Belt, Only 65c.

HE 110 Men's Smooth Cowhide Belt, 2½ in. wide, with nickel plated 2-prong harness buckle; watch pocket and coin pocket with button lock; orange color only. Sizes, 22 to 46 in. Mention waist measure when ordering. Shipping weight, 7 oz. Our price only.......... **65c**

Combination Game Board.

HE 543 "Star Archareus" Combination Game Board No. 1, and revolving stand, with 60 interesting and instructive games; 29 in. square; elegant moulded hard-wood rim, finished imitation mahogany; 3-ply maple veneer panel in natural finish. Diagrams in two colors. Attractive, moderate in price, and very popular. Retail price, $2.25. Shipping weight, 15 lbs. Our price, only.......... **$1.65**

Mammoth Value Stationery Box, Only 38 Cents.

HE 704 "Madison" Bond Cabinet Papeterie Box, containing 100 sheets "Royal" size 6x6⅜-in. note paper in three tints, with oblong envelopes to match. Retail value, one dollar. Shipping weight 40 oz. Per box.. **38c**

"Peggy From Paris" Hand Bag.

HE 425 Woman's "Peggy from Paris" Hand Bag of tan colored plaited grained leather, 6 in. deep, 3 in. long. Gilt metal frames with fancy ball catch and two flat leather covered handles. Colored moire silk lining. Fitted with card case and coin purse of leather to match bag. Shipping weight, 12 oz. Each .. **$1.50**

"Auto" Hand Bag.

HE 339 Woman's Auto Hand Bag, of black steer grained leather, 4½ in. deep, 9 in. long. Fancy gilt frame with ball catch and braided leather handle. Colored moreen lining. Fitted with smelling salts bottle, card case and coin purse of leather to match bag. Shipping weight, 14 oz. Each .. **$1.50**

Millinery Bargains

Our Millinery is strictly up-to-the-minute, the very newest and most up-to-date styles.

Those accustomed to paying fancy prices for Millinery will be surprised at our values. Millinery materials at wholesale are not expensive. What the milliner charges you for is her "Art." It's all plain business with us. We buy the materials in large quantities at lowest prices, figure in the trimmer's time at so much per hour, and you get the hat direct with but one regular small profit and costing you about one-half what a local milliner would charge.

YE 640

YE 658

YE 680—"Macbeth." A pretty draped turban over a buckram frame, fancy shirred rosettes
YE 680

YE 640—"Cassie." An other pretty mode made of soft silk tucked and draped over a buckram frame with a plain covered velvetta crown, two long ostrich plumes around fronts and sides, caught at right side with a pretty gilt and steel buckle and large bow of wide satin taffeta ribbon with draw over to back finished with a bow. Black only. Wt. 4 oz. Price.... **$3.75**

YE 658—"Elia." Crushed silk velvet hat, large brim and high crown, has bandeau at front giving hat the proper tilt. The hat is covered in silk crushed velvet with plain silk velvet binding, three handsome plumes at side of crown falling over edge of brim, wide satin taffeta ribbon bow under brim and draw on top with steel and gilt buckle at back. Hat comes in black, brown or navy. Weight, 6 oz. Each................... **$4.65**

YE 678—"Viola." A made turban, a pretty new style, pointed front and close back, frame covered with fine velvetta, three ostrich tips at side, two gilt buckles in front and satin taffeta ribbon over front and crown knotted at back. Hat in black only, ribbon in all colors. Wt. 6 oz. Price............ **$1.35**

YE 678

In the velvet and heavy lace over top and sides, bandeau around front and fancy feather ornaments at side with taffeta ribbon brought from right side over top and caught with two gilt button ornaments at left side. Comes in all colors. Wt., 4 oz. Each.. **$2.00**

Golden Harvest Dinner Set 4 95

100 Pieces

Golden Harvest Dinner Set

One of the Greatest Bargains You Ever Saw

Description Body is a high grade of American semi-porcelain, pure white, heavily glazed and guaranteed not to surface crack or craze. The shapes are perfect in every detail, designed by one of the best modelers in the country. Great attention has been given to artistic effect. The beauty of the graceful shapes has been greatly enhanced by the dainty embossing following the edges of all the pieces. This is a Full Hundred Piece Selected Dinner Set at the price usually asked for seconds, and the extra value will be readily recognized by all good judges of dinner ware. Remember, the price is for a full dinner set, as per following assortment. Weight, packed ready for shipping, 90 lbs.

This Quality Would Cost Elsewhere Almost Double

12 Tea Cups
12 Tea Saucers
12 Pie Plates, 7¼ in., actual measure
12 Tea Plates, 8¼ in., actual measure
12 Diner Plates, 9¼ in., actual measure
12 Sauce Dishes
12 Individual Butters

1 Platter, 8 in.
1 Platter, 12 in.
1 Oval Open Veg. Dish
1 Round Open Veg. Dish
1 Covered Dish, 8 in.
1 Covered Butter and Drainer

1 Covered Sugar Bowl
1 Cream Pitcher
1 Gravy Boat
1 Pickle Dish
1 Pitcher, 1 qt.
1 Bowl, 1½ pt.

4 95

100 Pieces

Order Number BE 55. The Golden Harvest Dinner Set for

Perfect Protectors

Happy hands are those inside of our Gloves. Order from us everything your family needs in Gloves and Mittens. You cannot do as well elsewhere.

Children's and Misses' Golf Gloves

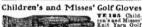

YE 185 Children's and Misses' Knit Yarn Golf Gloves; come in red, navy blue, gray, white and black, with fancy combination colored stripe centers. Sizes, from 8 to 16 years. Per dozen pairs, $2.70. Per pair.................**25c**

YE 186 Misses' and Children's Solid Colored Golf Knit Yarn Gloves; derby ribbed, close fitting. Colors, red, navy blue, white, gray and black. Sizes, from 8 to 16 years. Per pair.......**40c**

Ladies' Golf Gloves

YE 187 Ladies' Knit Yarn Golf Gloves, soft and warm, and will be much in demand this season. Come in the following colors: Gray, red, navy blue, white and black, with mixed combination centers. Per dozen pairs, $2.70. Per pair..............**25c**

YE 188 Ladies' heavy Knit Derby Ribbed Golf Gloves. These gloves are very heavy and warm. Colors, red, gray, navy blue, white and black, with fancy centers of combination colors. Per pair........**45c**

YE 191 Ladies' Fancy Knit Golf Gloves, made with a long wooly gauntlet, making a good warm glove; come in the following combinations: Black with white stitching on backs, cream with black stitching on backs, gray with black and white stitching on backs, and made with white and black stitching on backs, and shaded combination gauntlets. Weight 2 oz. Per dozen pairs, $5.40. Per pair................**50c**

Ladies' Lined Kid Gloves

YE 270 Ladies' Dressed Kid Gloves, heavy fleece lined, black French coney fur top, with patent snap clasp at wrist, three rows of stitching on back, over seam, inserted glove thumb, gusseted between fingers, making a good warm durable glove for driving or walking. Colors, brown and tan only. Sizes, 6 to 8½. Per pair..................**$1.00**

Ladies' Deer Skin Gloves

YE 142 Ladies' Genuine Deer Skin Gloves, suede or undressed finish, the natural fur is on the inside of gloves in place of lining, making the glove much warmer and a better fit. With two snap clasps at wrist and 3 rows stitching on back. Sizes, 6 to 8. Color, dark brown. Wt., 2½ oz. Pair, **$3.00**

Ladies' Brown Mocha Mittens

YE 265 Ladies' Brown Mocha or undressed kid Mittens, black French coney fur around top, patent snap clasp at wrist, over seam, inserted glove thumb, fleece wool lined, three row stitched backs. Sizes, 6 to 8½. This is a handsome and warm mitten. Per pair...............**50c**

YE 266 Ladies' Black Mocha or undressed kid Mittens, one snap clasp at wrist, overseam stitched and gusseted between thumb, three rows pique stitching on back, two rows of stitching around wrist and on both sides of opening in front. This is a very neat, warm and durable mitten for ladies, the wool fleece lining makes this mitten very desirable. Black only. Sizes, 6 to 8½. Per pair..**$1.00**

YE 268 Ladies' New Alaska Mittens; astrakhan cloth back, wrist and gauntlet, kid front, heavy wool fleece lined, one snap clasp at wrist; the gauntlet is 4 inches wide and lined with lambskin, making a good warm mitten for driving or walking. Black and brown only. Sizes, 6 to 8½. Per pair..**$1.00**

Ladies' Dressed Kid Gloves

YE 110 Ladies' 2-Clasp Kid Gloves "Thornward," the latest 3-row silk embroidered backs. This is the strongest and best glove in the market for the price, and every pair is a perfect fit. Colors, brown, tan, mode, slate, white and black. Sizes, 6 to 8. Weight, 3 oz. Per pair.....................**$1.00**

Ladies' Flannelette Night Dresses or Robes

Warm and Serviceable Garments at Wholesale Prices

YE 756   YE 798   YE 803   YE 803   YE 800   YE 806

Every Robe

Exactly as described, and of better material than the same money would buy elsewhere.

These garments are particularly warm and comfortable, and very desirable for fall and winter weather. Made in regular sizes only. Neck, 14, 15, 16. Bust, 32, 34, 36, 38, 40, 42.

YE 796 Ladies' Fancy Striped Flannelette Night Dresses, made full, with pointed collar. Mother Hubbard style yoke in front, or back made double thickness, wide double cuffs at the wrist. Yoke, collar and cuffs are trimmed with one row of fancy braid to match night dress. Colors: Cream with light blue stripes, or cream with pink stripes. Length, about 54 in. Size, 14, 15 & 16 in. neck. Weight, 14 oz. Per doz.......$5.40 Each...... **50c**

YE 798 Ladies Good Quality Fancy Striped Flannelette Night Dresses. This garment has a Mother Hubbard yoke in front and back, double thickness; front is trimmed with two rows of fancy braid running up and down and across, has turned down pointed collar with one row of braid to match yoke, also one row of braid around cuffs to match. The trimming on this gown is simple and arranged in a tasty manner. Colors: Cream and pink, or cream and light blue striped combined. Length 56 in. Sizes, 14, 15 and 16 in. neck. Weight, 15 oz. Per doz...$7.60 Each.. **70c**

YE 800 Ladies' Flannelette Night Robe or Dress, made of fancy striped flannelette, gathered yoke front and back, turned down pointed collar, and wide cuffs at the wrist; the collar and cuffs are made of solid color flannelette, in either pink or blue to-match stripes in robe, with 1 in. square of fine white Swiss embroidery inlaid at the points of collar and center of cuffs. Large pearl buttons and ribbon bow in front. Colors: Cream with light blue stripes or cream with pink stripes. Length 56 in. Sizes, 14, 15 and 16 in. neck. Weight, 19 oz. Per doz.......$9.30 Each...... **85c**

YE 803 White Flannelette Night Robes, made with gathered Mother Hubbard style yoke front and back, pointed collar and gathered flowing cuff sleeves. The yoke is made double in thickness and has a double stitched piece and pearl buttons in front, making an extra good garment. Comes in white only. Length about 56 in. Sizes, 14, 15 and 16 in. neck. Weight, 20 oz. Per doz.......$10.25 Each...... **95c**

YE 806 Ladies' Solid Colored Extra Fine Quality Flannelette Night Dress. Made Mother Hubbard style with square yoke in front and pointed in the back; has turn down collar and wide cuffs. The front of yoke has 8 rows of fancy braid running up and down and 1 row across. Cuffs and collar are also trimmed with 1 row of fancy braid to match yoke. This garment is made of firm twilled flannelette, both warm and durable, making a most desirable gown for Fall and Winter wear. Colors: Solid light blue or solid pink. Length, 56 in. Sizes, 14, 15 and 16 irk neck. Weight, 17 oz. Per doz.......$10.80 **$1.00** Each......

YE 806 Ladies' Fancy Striped Flannelette Night Robe or Gown. Made with a fancy double yoke front and back. On front of yoke there are four pieces of triangular shaped solid colored flannelette, inserted and bound with fancy braid to match. The collar is turned down and pointed, and also has one piece of solid colored flannelette on each side to match triangular pieces in front. The sleeves are gathered at the wrist. The collar, yoke and ruffle at wrist match stripe in gown. This is the latest and one of the most handsome garments in the market. Made full sizes and good length. Colors: Cream with light blue stripes, or cream with pink stripes. Length, 56 in. Sizes, 14, 15 and 16 in. neck. Weight, 19 oz. Per doz., $10.80. Each...... **$1.00**

All Wool Filled Ingrain Carpet

With Cotton Chain or Warp
Price, per yard
50c

Rope Portieres

Rope Portieres are very pleasing draperies and are used extensively where heavy curtains are not practical. They make a very handsome drapery for doors or windows where you do not wish to exclude the light. We show all styles and qualities in our general catalogue.

PE 003—The above illustration represents one of our best patterns of this grade of carpet in light chintz coloring which is the most popular color for this season. The quality is the best, only extra grade wool being used in its construction. It is claimed by many to wear as well as any ingrain carpet made. The weight is 20 oz. per yard. We can also furnish this grade in small or medium designs in reds, greens, etc. 36 inches wide. Per yard.................. **50c**

Rope Portieres

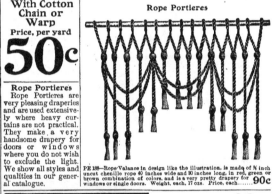

PE 186—Rope Valance in design like the illustration, is made of ¾ inch uncut chenille rope 40 inches wide and 30 inches long, in red, green or brown combination of colors, and is a very pretty drapery for windows or single doors. Weight, each, 17 ozs. Price, each....... **90c**

Moquette Rugs 98c

Ours are the handsomest low priced Rugs on the market.

PE 207—Moquette Rugs are without any doubt the most attractive worsted rugs made in bright colors. The pile is long and soft and the color combinations are exquisite. The illustration shows one of the patterns and we can furnish them in light medium or dark colors and in three sizes.

	1½ lbs.	3 lbs.	6 lbs.
Weight............			
Size in inches.......	18 x 36	27 x 60	36 x 72
Price each............	$0.98	$2.23	$3.96

Lace Curtains

Quality considered, we sell Lace Curtains cheaper than any other house in America.

Look at this beauty

Price, per pair.. **59c**

Novelty Lace Curtain
Very pleasing effect. Each **90c**

Battenberg Lace Curtain $1 95

A very neat and elegant pattern. Price, per pair..

PE 621—Lace Curtains with design like the illustration, of fair quality and finished with overlocked stitched edges. Each curtain is 36 inches wide and 3 yards long. The colors are white or ecru. We consider this number good value. Per pair 59c

PE 631—This is a novelty in lace curtains and they are very popular, as they make very attractive and impressive window draperies. They are a good quality, finished with overlocked stitched edges and are 68¼ inches wide and 3¾ yards long. They should be hung one to each window as shown in the illustration as the pattern is woven in the curtain, and the effect would be spoiled to attempt to drape it. WHITE ONLY. If they are not satisfactory return them at our expense. Price, each....................................90c

PE 663—These curtains are made of a good strong net with Battenberg insertion and edging, and a real nice bow knot ornament as shown in the illustration. This is a curtain that is strictly up-to-date and will give the best of satisfaction, as they launder nicely and are appropriate for any room. Each curtain is 40 inches wide and 3 yards long, in white only. Weight, per pair, 11 ozs. Price, per pair $1.95

A Solid Silver Berry Spoon. $3.00

NE 147—Solid Silver Cherry Blossom Berry Spoon. French gray finish ; gold lined bowl, good weight. Length, 8¾ in. Price.... $3.00 Postage extra, 9c.

26 Pieces Silver Plated Tableware $3.85

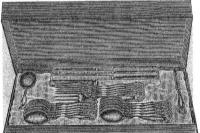

NE 457—Combination Set of 26 pieces of Silver Plated Tableware, in lined leatherette case. 6 Knives of Shell pattern, plated with 8 dwt. silver to the dozen. 6 forks, 6 tea spoons, 6 table spoons and 1 each butter knife and sugar shell of extra plate quality. Price of set comp ete............ $3.85
Weight, packed, 6 lbs.

Look at this!

A New Haven Clock in a Popular Mission Case for only $3.50

NE 625—This Old Mission Clock is made of solid oak exactly like the mission furniture now so much in use. It is substantially made, and fitted with the best 8-day New Haven movement, guaranteed a perfect time-piece. Is especially designed for use on the mantle or sideboard. Brown weathered oak finish. Polished brass numbers, hands and hinges. Half hour strike on cathedral gong. Height, 20½ in.; dial, 6 in.
Price............
Weight, boxed..21 lbs. $3.50

A Big Saving at Ward Prices

Men's Gold-Filled Watches, combining beauty with splendid time-keeping qualities.   Illustrations are exact size.

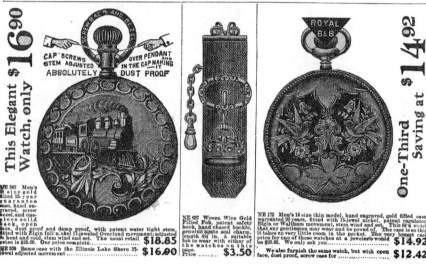

This Elegant $16⁹⁰ Watch, only

SCREWBACK AND BEZEL

CAP SCREWS STEM ADJUSTED — OVER PENDANT AND IN THE CAP MAKING IT

ABSOLUTELY DUST PROOF

One-Third Saving at $14⁹²

ROYAL B&B

NE 363   Men's E size gold filled 25-year guarantee case, hand engraved, screw bezel, and one-piece solid back, open face, dust proof and damp proof, with patent water tight stem, fitted with Elgin full nickel 17-jeweled Overland movement; adjusted to heat and cold, stem wind and set.   The usual retail price is $25.00.   Our price complete.................... **$18.85**
NE 369   Same case with the Illinois Lake Shore 17-jewel adjusted movement **$16.90**

NE 687   Woven Wire Gold Filled Fob, patent safety hook, hand chased buckle, genuine agate seal charm, length 4½ in.   A suitable fob to wear with either of the watches on this page.
Price **$3.50**

NE 173   Men's 16 size thin model, hand engraved, gold filled case, warranted 20 years, fitted with 15-jewel nickel, patent regulator, Elgin or Waltham movement, stem wind and set.   This is a watch that any gentleman may wear and be proud of.   The case is so thin it takes up very little room in the pocket.   The very lowest cash price for one of these watches at a jeweler's would be $20.00.   We only ask you........................... **$14.92**

We also furnish the same watch, but with open face, dust proof, screw case for **$12.42**

Here Are Two of Our Best Everyday Watches for Men

Not much show to them, but splendid timekeepers, most of the value being in the movements. Illustrations are exact size.

4-oz. Silver Case

17 Jewel Movem'nt $11.90

NE 840 This is a splendid watch, well adapted to the use of farmers or mechanics. The cases are 4 oz. solid silver, open face, screw bezel and back, with extra heavy crystals, guaranteed to stand 200 lb. pressure. The movement is the famous "Lake Shore," made by the Illinois Watch Co., of Springfield, and contains 17 selected jewels in settings; patent regulator, Breguet hairspring, adjusted to heat and cold, compensating balance, double sunk porcelain enameled dial, stem wind and set. A fine nickel movement, elegant in appearance, and guaranteed a perfect time piece. This watch cannot be bought from any jeweler for less than $20.00. Our price is only

$11.90

NE 878 Men's Full Length 1-30 Gold Vest Chain, soldered links, has drop piece for charm. Will wear for a life time. The makers will give you a new chain at any time this wears out. Price **$3.75**

NE 794 Men's full length good quality roll plate Vest Chain, with drop piece for charm. Price **$1.15**

Dust Proof Case

5½-oz. Silverine

$4.40

NE 874 The reliable 11-jewel Twentieth Century Watch. The best low priced watch made; has Breguet hairspring, compensation balance, jewels in settings, fine nickel and gilt damaskeen finish, and is stem wind and set. Case is the heaviest and strongest article of the kind in the market. 5½ solid silverine, dust proof, damp proof, and unbreakable. This is the best low priced watch in the world and is worth $8.00. Our price,

$4.40

We can ship either watch on this page by registered mail for 16c. We advise shipping watches by express, as express packages are more carefully handled than mail. Express charges on a watch to points within 500 miles of Chicago are 25c., to further points, 30c.

"The Best is Always the Cheapest"

Lakeside Sextuple Plate Silverware is the Best Value for the Money ever Offered

This is a reduced size illustration of our new Holly pattern Lakeside hollow handle Knife. The handle is hollow, full round shape to fit the hand; blade is fine thin crucible steel, hand forged and made to cut. Every piece of Lakeside ware is accompanied by a printed 10-year guarantee. The coating of silver on Lakeside goods is just double that used on the best Rogers' goods. Illustration at left shows the Holly Pattern Tea Spoon; Knives are full length, 9¾ inches, all other pieces in proportion. The handles are the new French gray finish with burnished blades and bowls. These goods are next to solid silver in quality and not very far behind. While we guarantee them for 10 years, we believe they will wear for a life time in the average family.

NE 283	Lakeside brand Holly Pattern Hollow Handle Knives, per dozen						$8.50
NE 289	"	"	"	"	Flat	"	Forks, " " 7.90
NE 289	"	"	"	"	"	"	Table Spoons " 7.90
NE 289	"	"	"	"	"	"	Soup Spoons " 6.20
NE 289	"	"	"	"	"	"	Tea Spoons " 3.95

Postage, per ½ doz. on Tea Spoons, 9c; Soup Spoons, 18c; Table Spoons or Forks. 17c; Knives. 25c.

Nothing Cheap but the Price

At our very low price for this good quality tempered steel Carving Set, every family can afford to own one

GENUINE STAG HORN HANDLE

$1.78

NE 995 Fine Quality Tempered American Steel Carving Set, ground to hold a keen edge in constant use, German silver ferrules, capped ends, 9-inch French blade, put up in fancy lined case. The best value ever offered for the money. This set will last for a lifetime. Others get $3.00 for this set. Our price (postage extra 38c)........................ **$1.78**

A Set of Shakespeare $2 10

Complete in 8 Volumes, Only

No Library is Complete without Shakespeare, the most noted, the most quoted of all Authors—the Greatest Writer the World Has ever known.

M E 800—The noted Falstaff edition, complete in 8 volumes, for only $2.10. Size per volume, 7¼x4¾x1¼ in. Weight, per set, 8 volumes, 10 lbs. The complete works of "SHAKESPEARE," containing the tragedies, comedies, all the poems and sonnets, and embracing a history of the early drama, an exhaustive biography, Shakespeare's will, introduction to each play, index to characters, glossary of obsolete words, names of actors and actresses of Shakespeare's day, notes on each play, etc., from the works of Collier, Knight, Dyce, Douce, Hunter, Richardson, Verplank, and Hudson. Edited by George Long Duyckinck, suitable for libraries, teachers, students, clubs, and homes. With 32 full-page illustrations, of which 8 are portraits of leading Shakespearian actors and actresses, and 24 are scenes from the plays taken from the famous Boydell Gallery. Handsomely and durably bound in cloth, red tops, with gold letterings. Publisher's price, cloth, **$2.10**

$5.00. Our price........................

Publisher's price, half morocco, $10.00. Our price........................ $3.65

Rare Values in Bibles at Remarkably Low Prices

Sunday-School Scholars' Bible for 89c

By mail, postage extra, 15c. (With Patent Index, $1.15)

Bound in Imperial Seal with overlapping edges known as "divinity circuit."

Contains in addition to the 812 pages of the Books of the Bible, 38 superb pictures of Bible Lands; 8 pages of colored maps and 168 pages of helps to the Study of the Bible.

ME 450 Features Worthy of Note:

FIRST—The convenient size (6x7), clear print, bound in neat, durable and attractive manner, of the best material and workmanship.

SECOND—The pictures of Bible Lands are one of the most valuable art collections published in any Bible and are really necessary for the proper interpretation of the Sacred Scriptures.

THIRD—Among the Helps is that incomparable feature, "The Four Thousand Questions and Answers to the Study of the Bible."

FOURTH—The maps are carefully prepared and printed in beautiful colors.

ME 450

The Largest Type Self-Pronouncing Family Bible

$1.10

A $4.00 Bible for $1.10.

ME 500—In addition to the 862 pages of the Books of the Bible it contains the following special features:

Chronological Index to the Bible.

Concordance to the Old and New Testament.

Self-Pronouncing Dictionary of Scriptural Names.

History of the Holy Bible.

Maps printed in richest colors.

Six full page colored illustrations.

Gallery of scripture illustrations containing 96 pages pages in black and white, and in addition many other full page Dore illustrations.

Marriage certificate. Family Record and Temperance Pledge.

The Lord's Prayer in colors.

Bound in imitation leather with full gilt sides, back and edges. Size, 10½x12½. Weight, 8 lbs.
The same Bible bound in genuine leather.
With nickel clasp, $1.95. .... $1.65

Our Leader in Teachers' Bibles

Bourgeois Type Self-Pronouncing Sunday School Teachers' Bible.

15 new colored maps. 4,000 questions and answers.

Size when closed, 6x9x1¾ inches thick. Printed from large new type on a fine quality of white paper, and contains in addition to the text, the Standard Helps to the Study of the Bible and 15 new maps. This edition of the Bible is indispensable to all students, teachers, Epworth League workers and Bible readers.

Note these Prices

ME 350—Bound in extra Egyptian Morocco, divinity circuit, overlapping edges, head bands and marker, round corners, red under gold edges. Retail Price, $4.00 .... $1.35

ME 355—Same as ME 350, with patent index $1.65

ME 236—Bound in extra French seal, divinity circuit, overlapping edges, lined with leather, silk head bands and marker, round corners, red under gold edges. Retail, $6.00 .... $1.55

ME 365—Same as ME 236, with patent index $1.80

Postage on Bourgeois Bibles, 25c.

Don't Fail

to examine the following List of Popular Books. You should at least have one to help you pass your leisure moments, and are all worthy of a place in your library.

ME 370 — The Greatest Detective Story Ever Written, "The Hound of the Baskervilles," by A. Conan Doyle. This edition has the same illustrations and the same sheet stock as the regular $1.50 edition. Our special price 45c

Postage 12c.

Our sales on "Methods of Lady Walderhurst," by Frances Hodgson Burnett, have been very large and we are now making a special price of, per volume 45c

"Lady Walderhurst" is one of the most charming characters in modern fiction. This edition contains the illustrations by C. D. Williams and with initial letters, tailpieces and decorative borders, by A. E. Wonralth.

Popular Fiction at Unusual Prices.

The best books and the greatest bargains ever offered at popular prices. Each bound in cloth. Our price, per volume 39c

Postage each, 12c.

Series ME 360—

The Virginian. Owen Wister.
Calumet "K." Merwin-Webster.
The Choir Invisible. J. L. Allen.
The Heart of Rome. F. Marion Crawford.
The Conqueror. Gertrude Atherton.
Pride of Jennico. Agnes and Egerton Castle.
The Crisis. Winston Churchill.

Don't Be Surprised

when we tell you that we have sold over 10,000 copies of Edward Noyes Westcott's great work, "David Harum," at 95c, and having now purchased a very large quantity we offer it at the low price of 45c

Postage 12c.

We have also purchased a large quantity of the following books, many of which are now being sold by retailers at $1.08 per volume. Our price per volume 45c

Postage extra, each 12c.

Series ME 375—

Aristocrats. Gertrude Atherton.
Audrey. Mary Johnstone.
Benefactress.
Beau's Comedy. Harper & Dix.
Castle Craneycrow. G. B. McCutcheon.
Cecelia. F. M. Crawford.
Confessions of a Wife. Mary Adams.
Dorothy South. G. C. Eggleston.
Graustark. G. B. McCutcheon.
Hearts Courageous. H. E. Rives.
Helmet of Havarre. Bertha Runkle.
House with Green Shutters. G. Douglas.
Janice Meredith. P. L. Ford.
Lazarre. H. M. Catherwood.
Manxman, The. Hall Caine.
Misdemeanors of Nancy. E. Hoyt.
Miss Petticoats. Dwight Tilton.
Mississippi Bubble. E. Hough.
My Lady Peggy Goes to Town. F. A. Mathew.
Mystery of Murray Davenport. R. N. Stephens.
Peggy O'Neal. A. H. Lewis.
Resurrection. Tolstoy.
Rockhaven. C. C. Munn.
Sir Richard Calmady. Lucas Malet.
Spenders, The. H. L. Wilson.
Tory Lovers. S. O. Jewett.
Two Vanrevels. Booth Tarkington.
Under the Rose. F. S. Isham.

Do Your Own Thinking.

Think of taking the greatest of all Encyclopedias and going carefully over every word, line and page, pruning out and eliminating everything that had grown obsolete by the lapse of time and adding to and supplying the latest word and figure on every subject of human interest, including hundreds of topics never mentioned in any other encyclopedia and you will have a fair conception of the wonderful value and scope of the 1904—

The New Americanized Encyclopedia Britannica

An Entirely New Edition. Revised Throughout. Fourteen Large Handsome Volumes.

Subscription Price, $39.00   Our Price, Per Set, **$12**⁵⁰

ME 595—It treats of 250,179 topics. Contains 37,204 biographical sketches; 36,680 cities and towns; the map of every State in the Union. The only strictly up-to-date Encyclopedia on the market now containing articles on the following and hundreds of other recent events, discoveries, inventions, etc. The tragic and lamented death of President McKinley, the Isthmian Canal Project, with the annulling of the Clayton-Bulwer Treaty and the proffer of French interests in Panama, American Military and Diplomatic Action in China, New Colonial Possessions of the United States, the Death of Queen Victoria, the Boer War in South Africa, Anti-Foreign (Boxer) Uprising in China, the

Visit of Prince Henry of Germany, Acquisition of the Danish Islands of the West Indies, Liquid Air, Wireless Telegraphy, Roentgen X-Rays, Lyddite, Trolley Railways, Automobiles, Polar Explorations, Alaska Gold Mining, Aerial Navigation, and the Santos Dumont and Zeppelin Air Ships, etc. This work has this exclusive distinction, that not only the supplementary volumes, but the original parent work has been revised throughout. Bound in half Russia leather. Gilt stamping. Over 10,000 pages, 100 colored maps. Each volume, size, 7 x 9½ x 2 inches. Weight, packed for shipment, 54 pounds. Our price, per set....:.... **$12.50**

Educate Yourself at Home $1 98

A combination offer: Webster's Common-sense Dictionary and two Courses of Study for
This Dictionary includes all the new words to June 1, 1902, profusely illustrated, over 600 pages. Size, 9x7x2¼ in. Weight, 3 lbs.

Select any two Courses from the following:

English Grammar.
English Composition.
French Self Educator.
German Self Educator.
Latin Self Educator.
Chemistry Self Educator.
Algebra Self Educator.
Modern Carpentry Self Educator—F. T. Hodgson.
Farm Engines, Easy Instruction Book—By Maggard.
Gas and Gasoline Engines, an Easy Guide.
Electricity for Home Study.

These studies are especially prepared for home study. The instructions are by some of the best educators. The books are prepared so that no teacher is necessary. There are no puzzling terms. Everything is fully explained.
REMEMBER—Our price $1.98 for one Webster's Dictionary and Two Courses of Study—your own selection. Each book bound in cloth. Weight per set, about 5 lbs.
Any one of these self-education books separately, 60c. each. Postage 10c.

THE GREATEST BOOK ON NATURAL HISTORY EVER WRITTEN.

Wood's Complete Natural History

ME 833 — The writer made a life long study of the nature and habits of every species of Wild Beast, Bird, Reptile, Fish and Insect known to man. There is not an error in statement in regard to any wild animal mentioned. There are hundreds of illustrations by Wolf, Zwecker, Weir, Coleman and others. One large volume, size, 7¾ x 10 x 2½ inches thick. Weight, 4½ lbs. Retail price, $4.50.
Our Special price..... **$1.45**

A Page of Popular "Pullers"

Every item on this page is a fast seller. A glance at the prices is sufficient explanation. They are useful helps which practically everybody needs, and nowhere else can the same quality be obtained at such low prices.

Include one or more of these with your order for our Cost Price Grocery Lot elsewhere in this booklet.

Anvil and Vise Combined

CE 760—Anvil and Vise Combined, with jaws for holding pipe; has chilled face and jaws; jaws are 3 in. wide; opens 5 in.; weighs 28 lbs. The base is of cast iron and is intended only for light work but will stand considerable hard usage. We do not, however, guarantee them again.t breakage. Each **$1.04**

Cast Steel Auger Bits

We recommend this bit for the use of farmers and around a house where a better grade of tool is not required. It meets the requirements of the mechanic as well. It is well made of good material and is warranted.

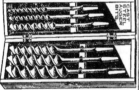

CE 870—This set consists of 6 Cast Steel Auger Bits, 1 each, ¼, ⅜, ½, ¾, ⅞, 1 in., packed in a neat wooden box. At the price we ask it's cheap. Weight. 3 lbs. Per set **87c**

Combination Tools

CE 826—This cut is an exact representation of this tool. It has a cocobola handle made extra large. The tools are all contained in the receptacle in the handle and are warranted the highest grade of cast steel. It has superior thumb nut and grip, nickel plated. Weight, 10 oz. Each **70c**

We have but 1,000 Sets of this fine Enameled Ware and cannot furnish any more at this low price. We therefore advise to order promptly.

Improved Wood Saws

Particular attention is called to the rods on these saws. They are greatly improved and will be found to be the best and strongest rods on the market.

Disston Wood Saw, 50 in.

CE 250—Selected maple frame, with No. 111 Disston round breast blade, extra thin back, new style steel, tinned rod. A practical wood sawyer's saw, and best made. Weight, 2 lbs. 4 oz. Each **75c**

Blue and White Enameled Ware Outfit $6.00 worth for

$4.90 Until all sold

Including a free copy of our Catalogue No. 73—

An excellent combination of cooking utensils in our High Grade Double Coated Blue and White Enameled Ware. Eighteen Pieces of utensils that are in almost daily use. They will make the housekeeper's lot easier and more enjoyable, as they are as easily kept clean as a china dish, are strong and durable, yet light and convenient to handle. Our Blue and White Enameled Ware is made from steel rolled especially for this purpose, which is double coated with a hard vitreous covering, presenting a smooth, highly polished and beautiful surface. The inside or lining is absolutely pure ALL WHITE; the outside is white, mottled with blue, which gives it a very handsome effect. Every article is carefully inspected before packing and we guarantee them to be free from defects, to be absolutely pure and safe to use and that there is no poisonous substance used in their manufacture. We have these outfits packed one set in a box ready for shipment and cannot make any changes in the assortment.

1 No. 8 Tea Kettle.	1 4-qt. Berlin Sauce Pan.	1 1¼-qt. Pudding Pan.	1 14-qt. Dish Pan.
1 2-qt. Tea Pot.	1 4-qt. Preserving Kettle.	1 3-qt. Pudding Pan.	1 1-qt. Water Dipper.
1 3-qt. Coffee Pot.	1 6-qt. Preserving Kettle.	1 12-in. Basting Spoon.	1 11¾-in. Wash Bowl.
1 3-qt. Lipped Sauce Pan.	3 9-in. Pie Plates.	1 3½x2⅛-in. Soup Ladle.	1 6½-in. Soap Dish.

Price for CE 50 Including our big Catalogue, Edition de Luxe, weight about 65 lbs. .... Shipping **$4.90**

Our
Derby
Oak

A quick

and economical heater

The Most Improved
20th Century Design
for
1904
and
1905

For
Coal
Only

$3.55

For
Coal
and
Wood

$3.82

Perfectly Air-tight.

Burns any kind coal or wood.

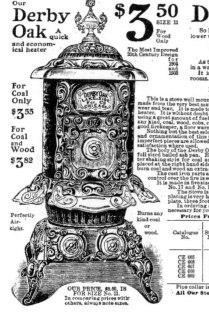

OUR PRICE, $3.50, IS
FOR SIZE No. 11.
In comparing prices with
others, always note sizes.

$3.50
SIZE 11

For Wood Only

Direct from Foundry

So low a price on as good a stove is possible only with us. This price is actually lower than the price most dealers pay. We handle thousands of stoves to their few.

This is the Lowest Price ever asked for this Stove
It Usually Sells for $5.00 or Over

As the illustration shows, it is not only very neatly finished, but every part is made in a way to give it unusual strength. Only the best material has been used in it.
It is also a **Clean Stove**, easily operated. No ashes or soot can escape into rooms. Ornaments are pure nickel and require no trouble to be kept bright.

Remember, We Guarantee it to do Everything We Say it Will

This is a stove well mounted by experienced mechanics. It has beauty of design and all the parts are carefully made from the very best material. Particular attention is given to those parts which have to stand the greatest wear and tear. It is made to radiate a great amount of heat and there is no skimping in the height or weight of this heater. It is without doubt the best Oak Heater for the money in the world. Many Oak Heaters radiate heat by using a great amount of fuel, but we have overcome that feature in our Derby Oak, as the smallest amount of fuel of any kind, coal, wood, cobs, chips or anything that will burn, placed in it will at once produce great heat. It is a good firekeeper, a floor warmer and fuel saver and it is made perfectly air-tight.
Nothing but the best selected pig iron, heavy sheet steel and highly polished nickel is used in the manufacture and ornamentation of this Oak Heater. Greatest care is taken in the mounting and fitting of all the parts. No imperfect pieces are allowed to go into it. We are selling thousands of these Heaters and all are giving the best of satisfaction where used.
The body of the Derby Oak is made of gauged polished steel. The ash pit bottom is sunken to allow the use of a full sized bailed ash pan. Heater has heavy, durable corrugated fire pot; the grate is strong and is of the draw center shaking style for coal and operates easily, can be shaken without opening the ash pit door, using the shaker placed at the right hand side of ash pit section; this will prevent ashes and soot from escaping into the room. To burn coal and wood an extra grate will be required and will be furnished at the nominal price quoted below.
The cast iron parts are made from the very best selected pig iron, the feed door is extra large, and perfect control over the fire is secured by draft opening in the ash pit door and check damper in feed door.
It is made in five sizes and the No. 11, No. 13 and No. 15 have only one screw draft register in ash pit door, while No. 17 and No. 19 have extra large ash pit doors, are furnished with two screw draft registers in same.
The Stove is equipped with a large swing cover ornamented with a fine spun metal urn. The nickel plating is very handsome and has a silvery luster and the nickel parts are as follows: Top band, name plate, three foot rails and screw draft registers.
In ordering always state the kind of fuel you wish to burn so that we will know the style and grate necessary for you to have.

Prices Free on Board Cars at Our Lakeside Foundry in Eastern Missouri.

Catalogue No.	Stove No.	Diam. of Body, In.	Floor to Urn. Base, In.	Floor Space, In.	Pipe to Collar, In.	Shipp'g Weight, lbs.	Price for Coal.	Price for Wood.	Price for Coal and Wood.
CE 665	11	10	35	16¼ x 16¼	6	70	$3.55	$3.50	$3.82
CE 666	13	12	36	18 x 18	6	85	4.55	4.50	4.69
CE 667	15	14	40	21 x 21	7	105	5.43	5.39	5.67
CE 668	17	16	43	23 x 23	7	145	6.80	6.75	7.07
CE 669	19	18	47	23 x 23	7	155	8.11	8.06	8.36

Pipe collar is 8 inches below base. No elbow required.

All Our Stoves and Ranges are Blackened and Polished ready to be set up and are Shipped Crated.

18 "Star" Tool Set $2.70
Standard Tools at the Bargain Price of

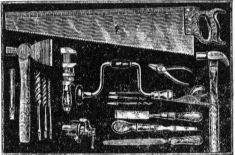

$**4**.69
to $8.94

The Most Economical Stove You Can Buy

$**4**.69 **Burns Anything. Keeps Fire All Night.**
More Desirable than a Base Burner. $**4**.69

Our Hot Blast Windsor Heater

Poorer Stoves are selling at retail for double our price.

This is a Wonder for Keeping Fire

This illustration shows our very latest design in a Hot Blast Heater. It has a front feed opening with drop door. This feature is entirely new in hot blast heating stoves and makes it unnecessary to swing the top cover to feed the fire. The great convenience of this device will be readily understood and appreciated. Is so constructed that it will burn any kind of coal, hard or soft, the cheapest grade of siftings, slack, lignite or coke, and requires very little attention. It will keep a fire a long time, and there will be fuel enough in same to heat the room for an hour or two in the morning without replenishing. Requires no more attention than a hard coal self-feeding base burner.

It is made from the very best grade of selected pig iron and heavy sheet steel, and to stand wear and give good service. It is very economical in the fuel it consumes for the amount of heat it radiates.

The body is made of heavy sheet steel; has heavy corrugated cast iron fire pot with cast lining above same, ventilated so as to admit cold air between the body and the lining through the front screw draft and discharging the heated air over the fire makes a smoke and gas consuming as well as hot blast heater. Has a large feed opening with drop door. Has draw center grate which shakes from the outside. The hot blast damper is operated without removing the swing cover. The ash pit is very deep to admit a full-sized bailed ash pan. The heater is elaborately ornamented; has a fancy swing top cover and elegant spun metal urn. The nickel trimmings are of the very latest design and are of the best possible quality. The nickel parts are as follows: Nickeled steel band around top, feed door, three foot rails and screw draft registers.

This heater is made in five sizes, and in the sizes No. 170 and 190 the ash pit door is large enough to admit of having two screw draft registers, while on the other sizes there is only one.

Pipe collar 8 inches below urn base.

Prices are free on board cars at foundry in eastern Missouri.

Catalogue Number	Stove Number	Diameter of Body, inches	Height, Floor to Urn Base, inches	Floor Space, inches	Size of Pipe to Fit Collar, inches	Shipping Weight, pounds	Price
CE 646	110	10	36	16½ x 16½	6	85	$4.69
CE 647	130	12	38	18 x 18	6	100	5.57
CE 648	150	14	40	21 x 21	6	120	6.25
CE 649	170	16	43	23 x 23	7	145	7.63
CE 650	190	18	47	23 x 23	7	165	8.94

Polished, ready to set up, and shipped crated.

Your Papers Are Safe
in one of our
Home Deposit Vaults

One year's rental of equal size space at your bank will pay for one of these Private Fireproof Vaults in the convenience of your own home **$7.70**

We offer here a steel fireproof vault that fills a long felt want in the home or office. They provide a safe place for your policies, deeds, jewelry, etc. Keep your papers and valuables private, and give positive protection against fire and water, sneak thieves or dishonest servants.

They are very substantially made of heavy steel plate, with steel hinges and draw bolts, and the locks are non-pickable.

They will never gather dampness, as do some safes, as the filling is perfectly dry; and the doors are fitted with a rubber gasket, which, in case of a fire, will fuse and seal the door, making it absolutely waterproof as well as fireproof.

At the low prices at which we are offering these vaults their cost is as nothing compared to the peace of mind and feeling of security that they give.

They are beautifully finished and shipped packed securely in a solid box, so that when delivery is made the contents need not be made known to those not concerned with your private affairs.

We include with each vault a certificate guaranteeing it to be fireproof and waterproof, and perfect in material, construction and finish.

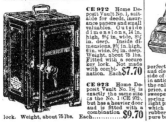

CE 972 Home Deposit Vault No. 1, suitable for deeds, insurance papers and small valuables. Outside dimensions, 14 in. high, 9¼ in. wide, 8¼ in. deep. Inside dimensions, 9¾ in. high, 6 in. wide, 5¾ in. deep. Weight, about 75 lbs. Fitted with a secure key lock. Not made with combination. Each **$7.70**

CE 973 Home Deposit Vault No. 1½ is exactly the same size as the No. 1 (CE 972), but has a heavier door and is fitted with a combination lock. Weight, about 75 lbs. Each **$9.70**

Our Improved
Handy Household Help

**M. W. & Co.
Scales,
Steel
Bearings**

$1.98

CE 700 This Counter Platform Scale has all steel bearings, heavy polished brass beam, and tin scoop. We warrant this scale to be accurate and reliable, and any scale proving defective in any way may be returned and we will pay expenses both ways. This scale will weigh 240 lb. by 4 oz. on the platform, and 30 lb. by ¼ oz. in the scoop. Shipping weight, 40 lb. Each **$1.98**

Made Expressly for Us
Carpet Sweepers

CE 790 The Ward Carpet Sweeper is a medium priced sweeper, made expressly for us by the largest manufacturer of carpet sweepers. Great pains have been taken to make it a perfect sweeper. It has perfect friction and the dust pans are easily opened and cleaned. A rubber band extends around the outside of case to protect furniture. The case is finished in antique oak, handsomely decorated. It is positively the only broom action carpet sweeper ever sold at our price, and the only device invented which makes the sweeper self-adjusting to every kind of carpet. Its spring dumping device opens both pans by a single light pressure. It has our automatic reversible bail, which holds the sweeper always firmly on the carpet, rubber frictions, rubber furniture protector, and our pure bristle everlasting brush. The cases are made of

---

popular woods handsomely hand decorated. The construction is as perfect as care and skill can make it. Each sweeper is carefully tested and fully guaranteed. Weight, 6 lbs. Each **$1.85**

Practically Everlasting. The Great Labor Saver—Wringwell Iron Frame Wringer
WARRANTED TWO YEARS

CE 738 Wringwell Wringer with iron frame and self-adjusting steel springs. One of the most popular wringers we have. Fitted with a good quality of white rubber rolls, size 10 x 1¾ in. Warranted two years for family use. Frame is made entirely of metal, including the apron or clothes guide which is thoroughly galvanized to prevent rust. Simple and substantial in construction. Each **$1.75**

Worth Many Times its Cost
as a Kitchen Convenience
"Gem" Food Chopper

CE 495 Gem Food and Meat Chopper. Will chop meat both raw and cooked, vegetables, fruit, bread, eggs, nuts, figs and other foods. Works easily, and will chop coarse or fine in uniform pieces without meshing, tearing or grinding. It lessens your kitchen work, and will prove useful every day in the year. Handsomely tinned, self-cleaning and self-sharpening. Four cutters with each chopper for cutting coarse, medium, fine and pulverizing, and we also include a cutter for nut-butter. Weight, 5 lbs. Each **80c**

Every Woman Likes Them
Very cheap at our price...**65c**

Mrs. Potts'
Sad Irons

This cut represents a full set of three irons, one stand and one detachable walnut handle.

CE 750 Extra polished; weight, per set, 15 lbs. Per set **65c**
CE 751 Nickel-plated. Per set, 68c

Unusual Values in Ready Made Clothing

See Sample Book Coupon on Another Page.

Everyone of them we think particularly attractive and of special value, and from the way they are ordering, many of our customers evidently agree with us.

Round cut sack style.

WE 59—Medium Weight Fancy Worsted Suit. Made from one of Wallack Heorters fancy mixed worsteds and is an ideal business suit. The pattern is a mixture of dark blue and brown, woven into a small herring bone stripe effect and there is also a slight mixture of white silk. Suit is made with fine quality Mohair Serge linings. It is a regular $15.00 suit and the only reason we can sell it at so low a price is because we manufacture the garments in large quantities ourselves, thereby saving the regular jobbers' prices. A great saving in this number. Suit, style 1, Round Cut Sack only. **$10.50** Price...

WE 25—Very Heavy All Wool Cassimere Suit. The fabric has a plain surface with a rather rough, woolly finish, similar to a Freize in appearance though not so heavy weight. A medium dark brown mixed pattern very appropriate for every day business wear. The suit is well made with good quality of Italian body lining, twill sleeve lining, and we can furnish in either single or double breasted sack style. This is a good, warm and durable suit, one of the extraordinary values in our Ready Made stock, and is about the same quality as is usually sold for $9.00

Suit, Style 1, Single Breasted. Price..... **$6.00**   Suit, Style 3, Double Breasted. Price..... **$6.50**

SEE SAMPLE BOOK COUPON ON ANOTHER PAGE

Rain Coats and Mackintoshes

Rain Coats are now very popular for both men and women. We are headquarters for all the latest styles and best values. We quote here several of our most desirable numbers—other styles and prices shown in Special Catalogue 73.

Sizes, Men's Raincoats 36 to 48 Chest measurement.
Sizes, Women's Raincoats 34 to 42 Bust measurement.

SEE SAMPLE BOOK COUPON ON ANOTHER PAGE

The Brunswick

WE 706—This Stylish Rain Coat of fine twilled fancy worsted made in very latest style and perfectly tailored. Has the new military collar; full cape, trimmed with plaits and with cloth covered buttons, Princess sleeve with fancy cuff, side pockets slit, semi-fitting back, and full belt. There is genuine satisfaction in buying a garment that is absolutely new, perfect fitting and possesses all the good features of the highest price Rain Coats. We consider this an excellent value and are confident it will give entire satisfaction. We offer this in the most popular colors, medium tan and Oxford gray. Price... **$11.00**

WE 708—Women's Rain Coat, same style exactly as preceding number, of a very fine grade diagonal worsted, smooth surface with medium width diagonal wale. Heavier weight than preceding number, has fine quality Venetian lining in back, and can be worn winter or summer. This coat is sold for $20.00 everywhere. It surpasses anything of the kind we have ever quoted and we feel confident that this exceptional value will be appreciated by our customers. It is the most fashionable style, perfectly tailored, and possesses every feature of the highest priced Rain Coats. Colors are very rich light tan and Oxford gray. Woman's Rain Coat, price....... **$13.50**

WE 606—Men's "Devonshire" Style Mackintosh of fine grade wool worsted with very fine pin check on black ground, has a dressy appearance. For well dressed men who want something more waterproof than a rain coat. Here you have durability, style, protection, and a coat you can wear any season of the year. Absolutely wind, dust and shower proof. Contains every important feature of a mackintosh and is perfect fitting. Has lining same appearance as outside cloth and first-class proofing. Don't pay $12.00 for a mackintosh when you can buy the best for ⅓ less. Average length 52 inches. Price....................................... **$8.00**

WE 706 — WE 708

Men's Workday Clothing

What a satisfaction it is to be properly attired for your work, no matter what may be the nature thereof. If you are occupied with heavy, rough work, subjected to the cold, bleak winds, snow or rain, you should be attired in extra heavy garments made of material of the right texture. Here we have them. Pick out any single garment or, better yet, order the Coat, one of the Vests and Trousers and you will have the warmest, the best and most sensible and practical suit for rough, heavy winter work you ever purchased, and at a moderate cost.

Men's Double Breasted Russian Vests.

Sizes: 36 to 48 chest measure. Average actual weight. 2 lbs.

WE 313 — Very heavy, rough surface, all-wool Cassimere or Dickey Kersey cloth, dark gray plaid effect, similar to WE 309 coat and WE 009 trousers. Made in double-breasted style to button close up to the throat, with two rows of six each black ivory buttons, and has four outside pockets. Lined throughout with a heavy-weight gray cassimere, closely resembling a wool jeans, and interlined with textile buckskin, a fabric that no wind or cold can penetrate. This garment is a thorough lung protector and is one of the most practical workingman's vests in the market. Price.................. **$2.00**

Men's All-Wool Dickey Kersey Trousers.

WE 109 — Men's All-Wool Dickey Kersey Trousers. This is a heavy-weight fabric, has a rather rough surface, but firmly woven and is well known on account of its great wearing qualities. The trousers are extra well made, have strongly sewed seams, patent riveted buttons and side pockets. The pattern is a rich, dark oxford gray, with a large overplaid formed by narrow stripes of red and dark green, which run either way across the surface about two inches apart, not loud or conspicuous but just enough color to take away the plainness of a solid oxford. The shade matches exactly WE 309 Reefer and WE 313 Russian Vest quoted on this page. These three garments taken together would make a very practical, warm and sightly suit for the workingman.

Price, trousers only..................	**$1.75**
Price, WE 309—Coat..................	4.25
Price, WE 313—Vest..................	2.00
Price of whole suit..................	8.00

Men's All-Wool Dickey Kersey Reefer.

WE 309—An all-wool fabric containing more than ordinary wearing qualities and extra heavy weight. It is firmly woven and has a rather rough, woolly finish.

Made up in double-breasted reefer style with a fire inch ulster collar with throat tab to match. Has three outside pockets with flaps and is lined throughout with a heavy gray wool flannel. This garment together with WE 313 vest and WE 811 or WE 109 trousers would make an excellent suit for a workingman who wishes something neater than a common duck. They would insure him warmth and comfort that he would not get from any other woolen garments, and the general appearance of the suit would suggest something better than common working garments. Average actual weight, 4½ lbs.
Price, Reefer Coat, only.................. **$4.25**

Men's Heavy Weight All-Wool Rain Proof Trousers.

Sizes: 30 to 42 waist measure. 30 to 36 inseam measure. Average actual weight, 2¾ lbs.

WE 811 — Heavy weight all-wool Cassimere, a very closely woven compact fabric and is one of the best wearing materials ever made into trousers. Color dark oxford gray. The fabric has been proofed by the best known chemical process and is nearly impervious to water. It will not absorb the moisture, but if the water is forced through the cloth by a heavy, driving rain, it can easily be shaken out and will not retain any of the moisture in the fabric. These trousers, therefore, will give the protection against wind, wet and cold which no other woolen trousers can. Made with two side, two hip and one watch pockets, patent riveted buttons and double-stitched seams, which will never rip. These trousers, together with WE 309 coat and WE 313 vest, would make an excellent wearing suit, and would afford the wearer warmth and comfort in the most severe weather.
Price, Trousers only.................. **$3.50**

A Few of our Very Strong Values in Overcoats

Sizes, all 35 to 44 chest.

Our Special Blue Kersey Dress Overcoat

WE 211—Fine Quality Dark Blue Kersey Overcoats. Our great special value at $8.50. The fabric is a genuine strictly all-wool dark blue kersey, full heavy weight, about 28 ounces to the yard, which is the heaviest made for dress overcoats of this kind. The body is very compact in weave while the surface is perfectly smooth, hardly any nap noticeable even by rubbing against the weave. The edges are finished raw with two rows of fine stitching. Edges of pocket flaps and all seams are finished the same. The body lining is of heavy double warp leather Italian cloth and sleeves lined with lusterine which is really the very best wearing sleeve lining that is made for overcoats. Coat has two-inch wide velvet collar, and is perfectly finished in every detail. If you buy one of these coats and do not think it would retail generally for $12.50 or more you may return it at our expense. We have contracted for a great many hundred, all we think we can use, but we sometimes underestimate the demand—so send your order early. Overcoat style 9 .... **$8.50**

Our Special High Grade Oxford Kersey Overcoat, $13.50

WE 221—Very fine quality Oxford Gray Kersey Overcoats. These are finer coats than usually found in any ready made stock. We know our trade like good quality and that this is true in clothing is evidenced by the way orders are coming for this number. Made with raw edges and seams, mohair serge body lining, satin sleeve lining and fine quality velvet collar, nicely finished and well made throughout. You could not secure one of these coats in any retail clothing store for less than $20.00. Send your order now. Style 9 .... **$13.50**

Our Nobby Belt Overcoat, Style 15

WE 245—Made of a heavy weight all-wool fancy Cheviot in a golden brown and black stripe effect. This fabric has a rather rough surface, is a fancy weave and a good weight. Black, gray and golden brown are woven into a sort of diagonal or herring-bone effect, and this is divided every two inches by a narrow black and white stripe. Has also a large invisible overplaid of dark red, very subdued and indistinct. Has a very Scotchy effect and is an ideal fabric for this style of garment. These overcoats we make ourselves. They have double warp Italian body lining, lusterine sleeve lining and a removable belt in the back and are excellent fitting, neatly tailored garments. Average length, 50 inches. Weight, 7 lbs. Would sell at retail for $15.00 to $18.00. Belt Overcoat, price ...., **$11.50**

See Sample Book Coupon on next Page

Average actual weight, 7½ pounds.

Style 9

Style 15

Our Hat and Cap Division

is most complete, showing all the new styles at from moderate prices to the best. We show here a few of our new styles that are leading our list of sales.

Best Stiff Hat ever sold for $1.50

WE 502. Men's Full Stiff Hat in one of the most popular shapes of the season, striking in appearance, and becoming to either young or middle-aged men. Medium round crown, 5⅝ in. high, 2¼-in. brim. Trimmed with grosgrain silk band and soft leather sweat band. Good sensible hat, exceptional quality and a shape you will like. Color: black only. Price.................................**$1.50**

Our Klondike Driver for... 1 25

WE 744. This High Grade Driving Cap has no equal. Material is of the finest grade dark blue kersey, made with pull down fur lined band on outside. Nothing warmer made and affords perfect protection in the severest weather. Neatly trimmed with grosgrain silk and silk bow in front. Has cloth visor, forehead protector and made good full shape and well sized. Comes in dark blue only. Each.................................**$1.25**

40c Value Boys' Golf Cap 25c for

WE 770. Boys' Golf Style Cap, made from good quality blue cheviot. Has inside band of same material, 6-piece crown, 1¼-inch cloth covered visor and substantial lining, very neat, medium weight, and can be worn Fall or Winter. Color, dark blue. Per doz..$2.50. Price, each..**25c**

Our Special Pelt Mitten

WE 900. Men's Heavy Gauntlet Pelt Mittens, have genuine horsehide palms and thumbs, fleece lined, the cuffs are lined with melton cloth. Come in dark brown colors. Average length, 13 inches. You can't beat it. Postage, per pair, 12c. Per pair.................................**$1.25**

Fill in Coupon Below:

Just take out your pencil right now (never mind a pen) and check off like this (X) the Sample Book you want. Then tear out this page, put it in an envelope, mail it, and in a very few days you will receive, free of all charge, the finest Book of Clothing Samples you ever saw, and at prices that will surprise you. Just a pencil, one minute of your time, and it's all over. Do it right now, before you forget. Montgomery Ward & Co., Chicago:—Please send me Sample Book as checked. (Not more than two.)

MADE-TO-ORDER SUITS—Light Weight

....**Sample Book V 1.** Samples of Men's Medium and Light Weight Suits, made to order, from $11.50 to $16.50. Trousers, from $3.25 to $4.50. Also contains "Points on Dress," beautiful cuts of styles, tape-line, and full instructions for ordering.

....**Sample Book V 2.** Samples of Men's Medium and Light Weight Suits, made to order, from $18.00 to $30.00. Trousers, from $3.00 to $8.50. Otherwise same as V 1.

....**Sample Book V 3.** Samples of Very Light Weight or Hot Weather Clothing. Coats and trousers made to order and ready made. Alpaca and blue serge coats or coats and vests and blue serge and flannel trousers, ready made.

MADE TO ORDER SUITS—Heavy Weight

....**Sample Book V 21.** Samples of Heavy Weight Made to Order Suits, from $10.00 to $16.50. Trousers, from $3.00 to $4.50. Also contains "Points on

Dress," beautiful cuts of styles, tape-line, measuring blanks and full instructions how to order.

....**Sample Book V 22.** Samples of Heavy Weight Made to Order Suits, from $17.50 to $30.00. Trousers, from $5.00 to $8.50. Otherwise same as V 21.

MADE-TO-ORDER OVERCOATS—Light Weight

....**Sample Book 3.** Samples of Made to Order and Ready Made Light Weight O'Coats and Rain coats.

MADE-TO-ORDER OVERCOATS—Heavy Weight

....**Sample Book V 4.** Samples of Heavy Weight, Made to Order Overcoats, Pea Jackets and Ulsters, from $10.00 to $30.00.

MEN'S READY-MADE SUITS

....**Sample Book W 1.** Samples of Medium and LIGHT WEIGHT Ready Made Suits, from $5.00 to $16.50. Trousers, from $1.25 to $4.50. Also cuts of styles, tape-line, measurement blanks.

....**Sample Book W 2.** Samples of HEAVY WEIGHT Ready Made Suits, from $4.50 to $16.50. Overcoats, from $4.50 to $16.50, and trousers from $1.25 to $5.00 with cuts of styles, tape-line and measurement blanks.

....**Fancy Vest Card.** Samples of Made to Order and Ready Made Fancy and Wash Vests.

....**Corduroy Card.** Samples of Ready Made and Made to Order Corduroy, Moleskin and Khaki Suits and Trousers, and prices of fabrics per yard.

....**Mackintosh List.** Samples of Women's and Men's Mackintoshes and Rain Coats and Misses' and Boys' Mackintoshes, with cuts of styles, etc.

YOUTHS' AND BOYS' SUITS

....**Sample Book U 1.** Samples of Youths' and Boys' LIGHT WEIGHT Clothing, from 6 to 19 years, and illustrations and descriptions of Children's Clothing, from 3 to 8 years.

....**Sample Book U 2.** Same as U 1. In HEAVY WEIGHT Fabrics.

Name... Postoffice..

R.F.D... County... State.....................................

CPSIA information can be obtained
at www.ICGtesting.com
Printed in the USA
BVHW040855250119
538681BV00016B/343/P